Inside the World of Older Spouse Carers

Elaine Argyle

Inside the World of Older Spouse Carers

Elaine Argyle
Nottingham, UK

ISBN 978-3-031-61577-1   ISBN 978-3-031-61578-8   (eBook)
https://doi.org/10.1007/978-3-031-61578-8

This Palgrave Macmillan imprint is published by the registered company Springer Nature Switzerland AG.
The registered company address is: Gewerbestrasse 11, 6330 Cham, Switzerland

Paper in this product is recyclable.

PREFACE

Due to demographic and policy trends around the world, the incidence and intensity of unpaid care is growing, particularly amongst older people who are increasingly expected to assume responsibility for the care of themselves and their contemporaries. However, in spite of the widespread recognition in research, policy and practice of the significant role played by unpaid carers, this recognition rarely extends to older spouse carers who form the vast majority of the older carer population. As such, older people tend to be regarded as the passive recipients of care rather than the active providers of it. While care between older spouses is commonly seen as being normal, unencumbered by other commitments and not worthy of special attention, a view sometimes shared by older spouse carers themselves. This neglect is both reflected and reinforced by the fragmentation of research into unpaid care and older age. This has led to a lack of integration of knowledge between these two areas as well as the prevalence of a one dimensional approach to the topics being explored. Drawing on interviews with older spouse carers as well as relevant literature and statistics, it will be the purpose of this book to help to redress these omissions.

Nottingham, UK   Elaine Argyle

ACKNOWLEDGEMENTS

This book would not have been possible without the assistance of a number of individuals and organisations. These include the Economic and Social Research Council who helped to fund the research into older spouse carers, which is drawn upon in subsequent chapters [grant numbers R00429814265, PTA026270447]. Also playing a vital role is the information gained from organisations such as the British Society of Gerontology, the Office for National Statistics, Carers UK, Age UK, the International Alliance of Carer Organisations and the Organisation for Economic Cooperation and Development. Others who have helped in various ways and at different times include Lorna Warren for her research guidance, the peer reviewers who provided valuable feedback on the book proposal and Tony Kelly and the staff at Palgrave Macmillan for their advice on manuscript drafts. Finally, thanks must go to the older spouse carers whose experiences and perspectives are central to this book.

CONTENTS

CHAPTER 1

Introduction

Abstract It will be the purpose of this introductory chapter to provide an overview of the book. It will begin with an introduction to the world of older spouse carers and the different perspectives that have engaged in its exploration. This will be followed by an outline of subsequent chapters, their aims and content.

Keywords Unpaid care • Spouse carer • Older age • Older people • Structure • Action

1.1   THE WORLD OF OLDER SPOUSE CARERS

As a result of demographic and policy trends around the world, older people are being expected to assume increasing responsibility for the care of themselves and their contemporaries with the number of carers aged 65 and over rising much more rapidly than younger counterparts (Greenwood & Smith, 2016). These older carers currently make up around a third of the overall carer population and the incidence of caring progressively increases over the later life course with around one in five UK residents aged 85 and over performing a caring role (Greenwood & Smith, 2016; Larkin, 2017). The majority of these older carers will be caring for a spouse (Carers Trust, 2015; Greenwood & Smith, 2016) and the decreasing popularity of marriage is unlikely to diminish the significance of this

E. Argyle, *Inside the World of Older Spouse Carers*, https://doi.org/10.1007/978-3-031-61578-8_1

dyadic caring role with the proportion of older people living in couples projected to increase due primarily to improved life expectancy (Office for National Statistics, 2023).

Not only do older spouse carers form an increasingly significant proportion of unpaid carers but they are also likely to provide more intensive levels of care than other groups of carers (Greenwood & Smith, 2016), often while dealing with health problems of their own (Morgan et al., 2020). A further feature of the caring relationship between older spouses is the high level of interdependence commonly found within this relationship and a subsequent reluctance to seek outside help. This view is often shared by service providers themselves who may see spousal caring in older age as normal, natural and unencumbered by other commitments such as work or childcare and therefore not in need of support or intervention. This is reflected in the noticeable lack of service provision specifically aimed at older carers as compared to younger carers and is compounded by the low priority given to older people's services more generally (Larkin, 2017).

A similar neglect of the experiences and needs of older spouse carers has been apparent in research, in spite of the increasingly significant role that they play and the unique nature of this role. For when caring literature has focused specifically on older people, this is usually in their role as care receivers rather than as care givers, reflecting the perception of older people as the passive recipients of care rather than as the active providers of it. Furthermore, although some attention has been given to spouse carers, this has usually focused on couples who are below retirement age or of an indeterminate age and defined by the characteristics of the cared for person (Morgan et al., 2020). It can be argued that this neglect of older spouse carers is ideologically bound originating in the cultural and structural aspects of ageism and corresponding assumptions that older people are burdens and marginal to society (Phillipson, 1982, 2013).

Contrasting ideological and theoretical perspectives have also given rise to a fragmentation of research into unpaid caring on older age. This has led to a lack of integration of research in these two areas and the predominance of a one dimensional approach to the topics being explored. Thus, research into unpaid care has tended to be characterised by methodological divides, aiming to either 'describe and quantify' or to 'conceptualise and theorise' this experience for different groups of unpaid carers (Larkin et al., 2019). These divides have undermined a full understanding of the complexities of unpaid care and have been compounded by the individualised focus of much of this research. This has led to a neglect of the impact of the economic, social and cultural context on this caring and the social risks and the shared experiences that can arise from this (Morgan, 2018).

Similar divides have been apparent in gerontological research with different generations of thought, leading to a changing perspective rather than to an elaboration and consolidation of existing knowledge. Thus, first generations have tended to adopt individualised and medicalised approaches to older age, which attributes the disadvantage experienced in older age to an inevitable process of bodily decline. This has been challenged by second generation approaches which regard this disadvantage as being largely socially constructed. In contrast, third generation approaches emphasise the increasing incidence of diversity and agency in the third age of life, thus helping to counter to the perception of older people as the passive victims of adverse circumstances as preceding generations of thought tend to imply. As Twigg and Martin (2015) observe, these theoretical and ideological divides have begun to be challenged by perspectives which recognise the interplay between bodily decline, structure and action in the lives of older people. However, possibly due to the lack of integration between research on older age and unpaid care, this recognition has not yet been fully extended to the experiences of older carers.

1.2   Aims and Outline

This book will aim to counter the neglect of older spouse carers by recognising the unique and significant role that they play and by transcending the divided approaches that have formed a barrier to this recognition. Thus it will be argued that an integrated approach is required to understand their lives which includes consideration of activity and meaning on one hand and structure and constraint on the other. This approach should also incorporate elements of all three generations of gerontological thought and explore the multiple dimensions of unpaid care provision which have henceforth remained largely disconnected (Larkin et al., 2019). With this goal in mind, this book will present the experiences and perspectives of 26 older spouse carers. These were originally captured through in-depth interviews which were conducted as part of a UK-based ESRC-funded study (Argyle, 2003). They were then revisited in subsequent research including a further ESRC funded study (Argyle & Warren, 2005) as well as in the process of writing this book. This has allowed for the further pursuit of emerging themes with direct quotations from the original interviews featuring prominently throughout Chaps. 4, 5, 6, and 7 of the book.

The benefits of reusing qualitative research data in this way is being increasingly recognised (Hughes & Tarrant, 2019). For not only does it save time and resources, minimises respondent burden and maximises research visibility, it also allows for new interpretations and perspectives to be drawn upon. As such, since the interviews originally took place, the changing context of caring has led to ever greater demands on the role of unpaid carers and yet older spouse carers continue to be largely over-looked by research, policy and practice (Morgan et al., 2020). New perspectives have also emerged both relating to older age and to unpaid care which promote greater levels of understanding and insight into the lives, needs and experiences of older spouse carers and the influence of material, attitudinal and physical issues on these experiences.

In addition to the critical review of relevant literature and the use of carer quotes and vignettes, relevant statistics will also be drawn upon which will help to provide an international perspective, contextualise qualitative findings and uncover the generality of these findings. For, as Larkin et al. (2019) observe, the combination of qualitative and quantitative methods can help to transcend the long standing methodological divides apparent in research into unpaid care and take account of the dual nature of human experience. As it is not possible to give detailed coverage of all caring contexts, the main focus of this book will be on the UK but with some international reach and relevance. Indeed, as it will be shown, there are many similarities in the experiences of older spouse carers around the world, regardless of varying demographic, policy and practice contexts (Murray et al., 1999). There are also likely to be some overlaps in this context between the UK and other counties making it a useful point of comparison for international readers. The wide ranging focus of the book will also facilitate its breadth of appeal. For it is likely to be relevant to those with an interest in both older age and unpaid care as well as to policy makers, practitioners and researchers more generally.

Chapter 2 will provide an introduction to the topic of unpaid caring and the increasing significance of older spouse carers in performing this role. It will also review the development of research into older age and unpaid caring, helping to overcome the lack of integration between these two areas and locating them within contrasting perspectives on society and the state. Chapter 3 will begin with a review of developments in policy and practice and their implications for older spouse carers. It will thus be argued that in spite of rhetoric towards responsive and culturally sensitive service provision, their unique needs have not been recognised. This will be followed in the second part of Chap. 3 with an overview of the study which will be presented in Chaps. 4, 5, 6, and 7 and which will aim to further explore and illuminate the world of older spouse carers from the perspectives of carers themselves. The focus of these four chapters will broadly reflect the predominant themes of the successive generations of thought outlined in Chap. 2.

Chapter 4 will focus on the experience of caring thus reflecting the emphasis on 'caring costs' and later life decline apparent in early research into unpaid care and older age. In accordance with second generation approaches, Chap. 5 will explore context, resources and caring, examining the way in which the incidence and experience of unpaid caring can be socially constructed. This will be followed in Chap. 6 by a discussion of the way in which the caring role of older spouses is actively managed. Implicit in this discussion will be the recognition by third generation and postmodern approaches that older age can be characterised by activity and agency rather than by passivity and victimhood. A combination of themes will be drawn upon in Chap. 7, which focuses on respondent's access to support from outside the household. Chapter 8 will summarise preceding findings and will recommend the adoption of an integrated and eclectic approach to research, policy and practice. Drawing on examples of good practice from around the world, it will thus be suggested that, rather than 'reinventing the wheel', existing perspectives and approaches can be drawn upon in order to achieve this goal.

References

Argyle, E. (2003). *Caring and resources in older age*. PhD thesis, University of Sheffield. Retrieved May 24, 2023, from https://etheses.whiterose.ac.uk/5445/

Argyle, E., & Warren, L. (2005). *Older people and their money: Issues for policy and participation*, Cash and Care Conference, University of York. Retrieved May 24, 2023, from https://doi.org/10.13140/RG.2.2.13295.23209

Carers Trust. (2015). *Caring about older carers: Providing support for people caring in later life*. Carers Trust.

Greenwood, N., & Smith, R. (2016). The oldest carers: A narrative review and synthesis of the experiences of carers aged over 75 years. *Maturitas, 94*, 161–172.

Hughes, K., & Tarrant, A. (2019). *Qualitative secondary analysis*. Sage.

Larkin, M. (2017). Supporting caring and carers in later life. *Innovation in Aging, 1*(1), 1109.

Larkin, M., Henwood, M., & Milne, A. (2019). Carer related research and knowledge: Findings from a scoping review. *Health and Social Care in the Community, 27*(1), 55–67.

Morgan, F. (2018). The treatment of informal care-related risks as social risks: An analysis of the English care policy system. *Journal of Social Policy, 47*(1), 179–196.

Morgan, T., Bharmal, A., Duschinsky, R., & Barclay, S. (2020). Experiences of oldest-old caregivers whose partner is approaching end-of-life: A mixed-method systematic review and narrative synthesis. *PLoS One, 15*(6), e0232401.

Murray, J., Schneider, J., Banerjee, S., & Mann, A. (1999). Eurocare: A cross-national study of co-resident spouse carers for people with Alzheimer's Disease. *International Journal of Geriatric Psychiatry, 14*, 662–667.

Office for National Statistics. (2023). Census 2021 Statistics. *People's Living Arrangements in England and Wales*. Published 9 February 2023.

Phillipson, C. (1982). *Capitalism and the Construction of Old Age*. Macmillan.

Phillipson, C. (2013). *Ageing*. John Wiley and Sons.

Twigg, J., & Martin, W. (Eds.). (2015). *Routledge handbook of cultural gerontology*. Routledge.

CHAPTER 2

An Overview of Unpaid Caring in Older Age

Abstract This chapter will provide an introduction to the topic of unpaid caring and the increasing significance of older spouse carers in performing this role. It will begin with an overview of the incidence of unpaid caring both in the UK and around the world with particular reference to the experiences of older spouse carers and older carers more generally. There will then be a consideration of research on this issue. This will highlight the fragmentation in method and focus that has characterised research into both older age and unpaid caring, which has contributed to the neglect of older spouse carers and has undermined the full understanding of their experiences.

Keywords Demographic trends • Social gerontology • Dependency • Three generations • Diversity • Informal care

Caring between older spouses is not only one of the most common forms of unpaid care provision but the experience of this care also differs from that of other groups of carers and is characterised by such things as high levels of involvement, adaptation and interdependence (Johansson et al., 2022). These differences tend to transcend national divides with older spouse carers around the world sharing similar experiences (Murray et al., 1999). However, in spite of the significant role played older spouse carers and the unique nature of this role they have been generally neglected within the large body of research on unpaid care (Morgan et al., 2020). It will be argued in this chapter that this neglect is compounded by the fragmented focus of research into unpaid care and older age leading to a lack of integration between these two subject areas and the respective insights that they provide. Research has also been characterised by a diffuse focus and by methodological, theoretical and ideological divides which serve to undermine a full understanding of the experiences of older spouse carers as well as further marginalising their role. In order to redress these omissions it will be suggested that greater integration is required both in research and in policy and practice interventions.

2.1   A Unique and Hidden World

2.1.1   *The Incidence of Unpaid Caring*

According to the latest Census from the Office for National Statistics (2023a), unpaid care refers to the provision of help or support to a person with long term physical or mental conditions or illnesses or problems related to old age and excludes activities performed as part of paid employment. It is estimated that sixteen billion hours per day is spent in the provision of this care around the world (International Labour Organisation, 2018). This well exceeds the time allocated to formal care provision with eighty percent of all care in Europe being provided by unpaid carers (Eurocarers, 2023). Although definitions of unpaid care have become increasingly complex, incorporating a number of different dimensions, the unpaid caring role has traditionally been classified in terms of the tasks performed (Larkin et al., 2019). Thus in her seminal study of spouse carers below retirement age Parker (1993) developed a typology of caring activities based on a number of tasks including physical care, practical and social support, administration and supervision. However, Parker (1993) also recognised that the nature and manifestation of these tasks will vary greatly along the lines of age, class, gender and other social divisions, issues that have been further explored in subsequent research into unpaid caring which has emphasised the diversity of the caring experience (Larkin et al., 2019).

Diversity is also apparent in the incidence of unpaid care which is known to vary both nationally and internationally. These geographical variations in the incidence of unpaid care are well illustrated by statistics drawn from the Global State of Caring report published by the International Alliance of Carer Organisations (2021). It shows that the percentage of the population involved in unpaid care ranges widely from 5 per cent in Japan and Hong Kong to 21.3 per cent of the population in the United States. Although, these figures provide an interesting insight into the world wide incidence of unpaid care, they do have a number of drawbacks. An obvious drawback is that they provide a snapshot of the incidence of care taking place at a particular time and do not take account of variations in this incidence over time and between different regions of each country. Nor do they take account of international and organisational variations in measuring this incidence, the varying intensity of the unpaid caring provided or the characteristics of those providing it. Some greater level of detail is provided by the Organisation for Economic Cooperation and Development (OECD), which is a global policy forum aiming to promote policies that aim to improve the wellbeing of the international population. In their report on the provision of long term care (Colombo et al., 2011), they found significant international differences in the intensity of unpaid care performed.

Thus around half of unpaid carers around the world provide care for less than ten hours a week and this low intensity caring is particularly common in countries such as Switzerland (Colombo et al., 2011). This compares to Southern Europe where higher intensity caring is more likely with half of carers in Spain caring for twenty hours or more each week possibly due to the relatively low availability of alternative sources of formal support. Similar variations in the intensity of the caring role have been identified by the Census for England and Wales (Office for National Statistics, 2023a). This shows that out of a total of around 5 million residents providing unpaid care, the majority are low intensity carers, caring for nine hours or less a week (1.8 million) or high intensity carers providing care for fifty hours or more a week (1.5 million). While the incidence of low intensity caring has been found to be relatively widely dispersed, high intensity carers are most commonly found in Wales and in the North East of England (3.6 per cent and 3.4 per cent of the population respectively). Significantly, both the North East and Wales also have relatively high levels of social deprivation as well as high proportions of people reporting very bad health and disability as compared to the overall population (Office for National Statistics, 2023b).

In spite of its widespread and enduring prevalence, unpaid care received little attention until shortly after the Second World War (Purkis & Ceci, 2015). Since then this attention has progressively increased partly as a result of worldwide demographic trends and the projected increase in the number of those in need of unpaid care combined with decreasing numbers of people who can provide it. Thus, falling levels of fertility and the entry of women into the workforce will reduce the availability of younger family members to provide unpaid support with the working age population predicted to decline from 67 per cent in 2010 to 58 per cent by 2050 in OECD countries (Colombo et al., 2011). At the same time, due to increasing life expectancy it is predicted that those aged over 80 will increase from around 1 per cent of the world population in 1950 to 4 per cent in 2050. In some countries, this percentage will be even higher with Japan, Korea, Germany and Italy being predicted to have 15 per cent of their populations made up of the over eighties by 2050 (Colombo et al., 2011). Similar trends can be seen in the UK with the number of people in late old age rising more quickly than younger age groups (Cooper & Harrop, 2023). While the Office for National Statistics (2023c) has found that the number of people in England and Wales aged 65 and over has increased from 9.2 million in 2011 to over eleven million in 2021 with their proportions rising from 16.4 per cent to 18.6 per cent of the overall population.

The increasing demand for unpaid carer combined with the reducing availability of people to provide this care has been seen to be giving rise to a global caregiving crisis and a growing burden of dependency both in the developed and developing world (International Alliance of Carer Organisations, 2021). In order to measure this burden of dependency, the 'dependency ratio' has been developed (Harper, 2010). This is an age-population ratio of those typically not in the workforce, aged between 0 and 14 and over 65 and those typically in the workforce, aged between 15 and 64. It is used to measure the pressure on the productive population and the higher the dependency ratio, the more the working age population has to contribute to sustain its dependents. However, like the international inconsistencies in the measurement of unpaid care provision, there are a number of problems with this ratio and its relationship to the provision of unpaid care. For as Harper (2010) recognises, ageing populations do not necessarily lead to high dependency ratios if they are accompanied by falling birth rates and a corresponding reduction in dependent children. Nor is dependency and the need for care automatically linked to advancing years. For although the need for care tends to increase over the later life course due to the higher incidence of ill health and disability in older age, contextual factors, socio-economic status and proximity to death are also important indicators (Office for National Statistics, 2023a).

2.1.2   Older People as Care Providers

A further problem with the dependency ratio is that it assumes that older people are unproductive and dependent. Thus, in spite of alarmist claims of an impending caregiving crisis as a result of ageing populations, older people are increasingly likely to be the providers of this unpaid care rather than just the recipients of it (Larkin, 2017). Thus, future years are predicted to see an 'adapted intergenerational contract' in which, due to the high incidence of ill health and disability amongst their contemporaries and the absence of alternative sources of support, older people will assume greater responsibility for the welfare of themselves and others (Harper, 2010). This is upheld by recent statistics which show that, increasing numbers of carers are aged 65 and over and that they currently make up around a third of all unpaid carers around the world (Larkin, 2017). Similarly, within England and Wales, 1.2 million unpaid carers are aged 65 and over, with older carers forming around one in ten of the total population and with around half of these providing care for fifty hours a week or more (Office for National Statistics, 2023a). As such, older carers are much more likely than younger counterparts to be highly involved with women aged between 75 to 79 years and men aged between 85 to 89 years being the age groups most likely to providing intensive levels of care (Office for National Statistics, 2023a).

In spite of the significant role that they play, the issue of older carers has been largely neglected (Larkin et al., 2019). For when caring literature has focused specifically on older people, this is usually in their role as care receivers rather than as care givers (Qureshi & Walker, 1989). Although there has been some limited research into older carers, this has largely aimed to measure the 'burden' of caring or explore particular characteristics of the care receiver or the care giver rather than investigate the spousal caring relationship (O'Rourke et al., 2021). Omissions are also apparent in existing research on spousal caregiving. For this has usually focused on spouse carers who are below retirement age (Parker, 1993), of an indeterminate age or, as Morgan et al. (2020) identify, are of the 'younger old' age group aged between 60 and 75. The issue of child carers or 'young carers' has also received a great deal of attention in recent literature (O'Rourke et al., 2021). However, while estimates vary, these younger carers form a tiny fraction of the total carer population with a recent annual survey of UK based carers (Carers UK, 2022) finding that carers aged between 0 and 34 made up just 3 per cent of respondents. This compared to carers who were retired (26 per cent) and carers aged 65 and over (28 per cent).

Like the focus of literature that preceded it, this disproportionate attention paid to younger carers as opposed to older counterparts may be ideologically bound and shaped by the assumption that caring by older people, particularly between spouses, is normal and natural while caring by children is not (Larkin et al., 2022). It could also be due to the cultural and structural aspects of ageism in modern society, which is reflected and reinforced by negative stereotypes of older people and the assumptions that they are burdens or socially obsolete. Associated with this is a neglect of the importance of the marital relationship of older people due to their perceived marginality to society's mainstream projects of production and reproduction (Phillipson, 1982, 2013). However, from the relatively small amount of literature that is available on the specific experiences of older spouse carers it is clear that this differs substantially from the experiences of other carers, a difference that tends to transcend geographical and social divides (Johansson et al., 2022; Murray et al., 1999). It will be the purpose of the next section to further discuss the unique experiences of older spouse carers, the high levels of involvement, interdependence, isolation and adaption that characterise this experience and their neglect and marginalisation by researchers and service providers.

2.1.3   Older Spouse Carers

Some older carers will be supporting very old parents, adult children, grandchildren as well as friends, neighbours or wider kin. However, the vast majority, around 87 percent of carers aged 70 and over (Carers Trust, 2015), will be providing care to a spouse or partner and the incidence and intensity of this spousal caring role tends to increase over the later lifecourse (Greenwood & Smith, 2016; Morgan et al., 2020). The fact that such carers may have their own health problems is likely to exacerbate caring demands, giving rise to a 'double jeopardy' (Morgan et al., 2020). These findings have been reflected in a number of studies from around the world which have found that older spouses provided more intensive levels of care than any other group of unpaid carer and are often left in a precarious position practically, emotionally, financially and socially as a result of this caring (Ornstein et al., 2019; Turjamaa et al., 2020). The reducing popularity of marriage is unlikely to diminish the significance of this 'spousal' caring role whether it takes place within a traditional marriage or in less conventional dyadic caring relationships. For the proportion of the population living within a couple has remained relatively stable (Office for National Statistics, 2023c), and cohabitation outside of marriage is becoming increasingly popular for all age groups. Thus the recent census for England and Wales has found that, possibly due to improved life expectancy, the proportion of older people living as a couple has increased over the last ten years and they currently make up 60.7 percent of the older population (Office for National Statistics, 2023c). Accompanying the enduring incidence of the older co-resident couple is the breakdown of external sources of support and the 'adapted intergenerational contract' (Harper, 2010), potentially rendering the dyadic caring role ever more demanding.

Caring by older spouses is not only likely to be practically demanding, with such carers dealing, often in isolation with their partners progressively deteriorating conditions (Ornstein et al., 2019) but their attitudes and approaches to this caring are likely to diverge from those of other groups of carers. For example, the assumption of a caring role by older spouses is likely to be a gradual process which is assumed by default rather than through choice (Turjamaa et al., 2020). While the fact that this care takes place within a long-term relationship will in turn affect older spouse carers' approach to their role and their level of commitment to it. These approaches and attitudes may be linked to the normative expectations of living as a couple and, contrary to negative concepts of caring, can incorporate a number of positive aspects (Johansson et al., 2022). This is reflected in the benefits that older spouse carers report as deriving from their role including a sense of job satisfaction and purpose, companionship, mutual affection and the fulfilment of a sense of duty (Johansson et al., 2022). Due to the often mutual onset of disability and infirmity, these emotional benefits and co-dependencies deriving from the spousal caring relationship can be accompanied by a practical interdependence. While due to the limited nature of post-retirement incomes, material interdependence may also be more likely within these relationships.

In addition to the uniquely interdependent and intensive nature of the older spouse caring relationship is the transformation of the roles and responsibilities long held within this relationship (Andréasson et al., 2023; Morgan et al., 2020). This transformation will tend to involve a complex process of renegotiation in the performance of practical tasks as well as in the provision of decision making support, especially when caring for a spouse with dementia (Fetherstonhaugh et al., 2019). It will also necessitate the need to learn new skills (Morgan et al., 2020) and involve a blurring of traditional gender role divisions with the gendered nature of caring progressively equalising in older age. Thus while women aged between 65 and 74 years are more likely to be carers than their male contemporaries, this is reversed amongst the over eighties amongst whom men are more likely to be carers (Office for National Statistics, 2023a). Similar adaptation is likely to be required for spouse carers to come to terms with the onset of their partners, and possibly their own, increasing dependence and infirmity, and the 'anticipatory grief' that may accompany this (Morgan et al., 2020). Existing gerontological research suggests that this process of adaption in older age is often characterised by perseverance and the maintenance of dignity (Lloyd et al., 2014). Although research on this process of adaptation tends to focus on older people experiencing increasing infirmity themselves, it is likely that these processes can also be relevant to their spouse carers and are potentially magnified when both partners are experiencing this onset of infirmity. These attitudes and approaches can reduce the likelihood of such carers pursuing formal support or to even regard themselves as a carer (Larkin et al., 2022) which can, in turn, lead to greater demands in their role (O'Rourke et al., 2021).

In the light of the invisibility, isolation and interdependence of older spouse carers as well as the significant and stoical modes of adaptation adopted by them, it has been suggested that policy and practice should adopt a more culturally sensitive approach to service provision which should be embedded in and shaped by carers' own perspectives (Larkin et al., 2022). However, as it will be seen in Chap. 3, in spite of the advocacy of such cultural sensitivity, welfare policy and practice have failed to respond to this. The marginalisation of older spouse carers within welfare policy and practice has been reflected in research into unpaid caring which rarely focuses on their specific experiences and aspirations. This neglect has been compounded by the fragmentation of this research with its tendency to focus on different aspects of caring, serving to obscure the complex and multi-facetted nature of the caring experience (Purkis & Ceci, 2015). Further layers of fragmentation have been added by the lack of integration between literature on older age and unpaid caring and by the similar disconnect between different generations of gerontological thought and the respective insights that they provide. The next section of this chapter will explore these areas of fragmentation and will show that, like the wider demographic and policy context, research into unpaid caring and older age has evolved considerably over the years.

2.2   DIVERSE APPROACHES

2.2.1   *Methodological Divides*

Here, the 'problematisation' of research into unpaid caring and the methodological divides that have been apparent within it will be considered (Purkis & Ceci, 2015). Thus quantitative methods have attempted to describe and measure the experience of caring while qualitative methods have attempted to conceptualise unpaid care and explore its subjective experience for different groups of carers (Larkin et al., 2019). These divides have been reflected in similarly opposing views on the relative merits of the epistemological perspective of positivism on one hand and phenomenological perspectives and interpretivism on the other. According to positivist perspectives, it is possible and desirable for the study of the social world to achieve full scientific status. As such, positivists believe that, like matter in the natural world, human behaviour is a predictable and measurable response to external stimuli which can be quantified by means of systematic and objective observation and measurement. This positivist perspective can be seen to have had a great influence on much research on unpaid caring. Sometimes referred to as 'informal care', 'family care' or 'caregiving', such research tends to quantify the experience or costs of this care through the use of statistical methods (Larkin et al., 2019). An influential example of this is provided by Grad and Sainsbury (1968) who attempted to objectively compare the burdens experienced by the families of psychiatric patients in receipt of hospital or home-based care. They thus developed an overall rating of carer burden by evaluating the impact of caring on various aspects of family life, which were rated as 'none', 'some' or 'severe' and it was concluded that those providing care at home were more burdened.

While this research has paved the way for many similar studies from around the world on the costs of unpaid caring and the way in which these costs can be alleviated (Larkin et al., 2019), a number of problems have been highlighted. For as Purkis and Ceci (2015) observe, not only has subsequent research on the issue yielded contradictory findings but the goal of relieving carer burden has remained unfulfilled. This is partly due to inconsistencies in research design and the fact that, due to its narrow and largely quantitative focus, the multi-dimensional, dyadic and subjective experiences of those involved in unpaid care provision are largely overlooked (Larkin et al., 2019). For example, by confining respondents to a range of largely negative responses when questioned about their role, any positive aspects of their caring role and the incidence of mutual exchanges and interdependence within it are ignored. Also neglected is the potentially unequal impact of caring on different members of the families involved or on different categories of carers who are seen as a largely homogeneous group (O'Rourke et al., 2021). Moreover, rather than being objectively measurable phenomena, the experienced costs of caring may be socially or culturally mediated and reflect society's expectations about what carers should or should not be expected to do (Parker, 1993). These expectations may vary between countries, classes, genders and generations and may go on to affect the perceptions of carers, service providers and researchers alike of what is and what is not 'costly' as illustrated for example in the high profile given to child carers in spite of their very small numbers (O'Rourke et al., 2021).

The role of these issues in shaping the way in which researchers, service providers and carers themselves perceive the experience of caring serves to undermine the claims of positivists of the possibility and desirability of a value free social science. Indeed, adherents to phenomelogical and interpretivist perspectives believe that the techniques of positivism are inherently unsuited to the study of the social world. Thus it is argued that, unlike matter in the natural world, human behaviour is not a predictable and measurable response to external stimuli but is intrinsically meaningful and it is the role of the researcher to explore these meanings rather than attempting to copy the methods of the natural sciences (Purkis & Ceci, 2015). This meaningful aspect of human behaviour is apparent in unpaid care. For as Qureshi and Walker (1989) observe, it does not only involve the performance of tasks but also takes place in a relationship normally involving kin and as such, unlike formal care is closely related to such feelings as emotion and obligation. This distinction between formal and informal care is further emphasised by theorists such as Parker (1981), who have argued that, not only is informal care uniquely expressive in nature but it is also characterised by its idiosyncrasy and spontaneity arising from arbitrary factors such as the individual social contexts and life histories of those involved.

This growing awareness of the importance of subjectivity, meaning and motives in the understanding of human experience has led many researchers to entirely reject positivist approaches in favour of qualitative methodology. Coupled with this has been the growth of participatory approaches, particularly in the area of health and social care. Unlike quantitative methods, such approaches have been regarded as being intrinsically empowering, serving to minimise the existence of a research hierarchy and helping to emancipate participants rather than simply describing and documenting their situation (Beresford, 2002). In response to this, research into unpaid care has increasingly taken the form of qualitative studies focusing on the subjective experiences of caring rather than its objective costs. These subjective experiences are difficult to measure with quantitative methods and may have little relationship to the objective costs of caring but are of prime importance in influencing the way in which the caring role is managed and experienced. There has also been an increased focus on the differential impact of this care on different groups (Purkis & Ceci, 2015). Like earlier research, this focus has often been ideologically bound and is apparent, for example, in the large amount of feminist research into unpaid care (Finch & Groves, 1983; Milligan, 2005) as well as in policy documents on the apparent gender imbalance in caring responsibilities (Eurocarers, 2023).

In spite of the merits of qualitative research into the costs of unpaid caring, in focusing on the individual meaning and motives of carers, such methods overlook the way in which these meanings and motives are themselves constrained by objective social forms. For example, the spontaneous and expressive nature attributed to unpaid care by some theorists can itself be undermined by material constraint, having a subsequently negative impact on the quality of the experience for both carer and care recipient alike (Arber & Ginn, 1993). Similarly, in focusing on the individual as the source of all meaning and action, qualitative research tends to overlook the context of caring and the systematic differences and collective subjectivities that can arise from this (Tanner, 2010). Thus while people's actions are the result of their interpretations of a situation, their interpretations and choices are themselves limited by structural factors which are external to them and beyond their control. The participatory approaches commonly associated with qualitative methods can be equally flawed. For not only can they be tokenistic and give rise to 'consultation fatigue', they can also neglect the wider context of inequality within which the research takes place (Beresford, 2002).

2.2.2   *Contrasting Perspectives*

The methodological divides which have characterised research into unpaid care have been compounded by the significant theoretical and ideological divides apparent in this research both relating to unpaid care and to older age. These divides have led to a shifting focus of interest and perspective and can be linked to three generations of thought which are themselves situated within contrasting perspectives on society and the state (Wilding, 2018). There will follow a discussion of these three generations of thought relating to older age and caring, the way in which they intersect and the implications of this for research into older spouse carers.

For first generation approaches which were predominant during the period of welfare consensus, it is generally believed that care by the family is intrinsically preferable to that provided by formal sources. This view is linked to idealised views of the family and the care it provides, which is seen as combining 'caring about' as well as 'caring for' the person in receipt of this care (Parker, 1981). This consensual view can be seen as being allied to the traditional social administration approach to welfare and to the sociological perspective of functionalism. From these perspectives, the state and its agencies are regarded as the neutral arbiters of the public's wellbeing. While society is viewed as a complex but orderly system which operates to effectively meet the needs of the individuals within it. Due to this consensual view, it is thus believed that social problems are pathological, are attributed to inadequacies of the individual and should be dealt with accordingly through individualised approaches. For example, with regard to older people, social disengagement theory maintains that the disadvantage and social marginality experienced by older people can be attributed to their declining health, the impact of which can be ameliorated through such things as paternalistic welfare provision and medical interventions (Cumming & Henry, 1962).

These theories of the first generation have been challenged with the emergence of second generation approaches including the new social administration approach and conflictual concepts of society such as those expressed by Marxist and feminist theories (Wilding, 2018). From these perspectives, society is regarded as being inherently unequal and divided and is overseen by the 'capitalist' or 'patriarchal' state which aims to reflect and maintain the existing social order rather than to promote public wellbeing. In order to challenge this inequality, state employees such as social workers are encouraged to adopt 'radical' or structural approaches, which aim to achieve social change rather than solely adopting individualised approaches with service users (Phillipson, 1982, 2013). This conflictual approach is reflected in perceptions of the unpaid caring relationship which is seen as providing a less satisfactory but cheaper alternative to formal sources. With regard to its negative impact, it has been argued that providing care can be oppressive, a view particularly apparent in feminist research on the issue. This argues that in spite of women's large scale entry into the workplace, they continue to hold the main responsibility for this care in the home which is itself regarded as a site of female entrapment and male domination (Finch & Groves, 1983; Milligan, 2005). Similarly negative perceptions have been expressed on the experience of receiving unpaid care which the disabled movement maintains can also be oppressive, potentially serving to promote dependency and disempowerment amongst care recipients (Morris, 1993).

An important feature of second generation approaches is that it is believed that social problems are socially constructed rather than individually derived. This is apparent in political economy approaches to older age which, contrary to first generation perspectives (Cumming & Henry, 1962), regard the dependency and disadvantage experienced by older people to be largely socially created (Phillipson, 1982, 2013). Similar perspectives can be seen in situational constraint theories of poverty which attribute its existence to social processes rather than to individual inadequacies as earlier 'culture of poverty' theories had maintained (Lewis, 1998). In accordance with these approaches, it is increasingly being recognised that the experience of unpaid caring can also be socially constructed and influenced by contextual issues such as government policy, socioeconomic status and environmental factors. For example it has long been recognised that poorer sections of the population are more likely than better off counterparts to be in need of care due to their higher likelihood to experience of ill health and disability (Office for National Statistics, 2023b). The socially constructed aspects of unpaid caring can also be seen in the significant geographical variations apparent in the incidence of high intensity caring which is closely associated with the corresponding incidence of social deprivation, ill health and disability (Office for National Statistics, 2023a).

This social construction of caring has been further enlarged upon by the work of Arber and Ginn (1993) who highlight the 'ageless' and 'classless' analysis of research on this issue. Thus through the secondary analysis of official statistics they found that older and poorer sections of the population are more likely to be involved in demanding caring roles. In order to explain this differential, they use the term 'leverage'. Implicitly drawing on situational constraint and political economy approaches, this describes the way in which reduced access to cultural and material resources amongst poorer and older people can restrict choice in caring strategies utilised. thereby increasing the demands of the caring role. However, the suggestions of Arber and Ginn (1993) are speculative and based on the analysis of statistical data rather than on the perspectives of carers themselves. Nor do they take account of what subsequently developed third generation approaches regard as the increasingly idiosyncratic nature of unpaid caring or the increasing affluence, self-determination and diversity in the third age of life (Gilleard & Higgs, 2000). These third generation approaches can be seen to incorporate postmodernist perspectives on society which tend to reject the uniformity and grand theories adopted by earlier generations of thought in favour of heterogeneity, choice, self-identity and lifestyle. This is reflected in neo-liberal approaches to welfare which reject the false universalism of the post-war welfare state in favour of user led and participatory approaches, with employees of the state being regarded as the managers and facilitators of care rather than the providers of it. It is also reflected in perspectives on caring and older age.

Such perspectives place an emphasis on increasing diversity as individuals are released from traditional roles and expectations with unpaid caring becoming increasingly idiosyncratic and narcissistic and with older people having increasing power and agency. Thus it is argued that, contrary to earlier perspectives on older age, older people are not a homogeneous group or passive victims but that their behaviour is active and meaningful and is characterised by adaptation in the face of adversity (Gilleard & Higgs, 2000). It is thus claimed that even in the latest stage of life, attitudes of independence and stoicism tend to predominate (Lloyd et al., 2014). In order to avoid accusations of adopting an overly positive portrayal of later life and minimising the incidence of dependency and decline (Twigg & Martin, 2015), distinctions have more recently been made between the third and fourth ages of later life (Gilleard & Higgs, 2010). The former stage is seen as being characterised by a high degree of activity and agency. In contrast, the fourth age, which is shaped and defined by institutional practices (Lloyd et al., 2014), is characterised by the onset of illness, disability, dependency and ultimately death. This focus on bodily decline redresses a long standing neglect of this issue within social gerontology due to a wish to avoid the biological determinism of earlier medicalised approaches and has been further pursued in the concept of 'embodiment' within cultural gerontology (Tulle, 2015). As the name suggests, this focuses on the bodily ageing and the meanings and strategies attached to it.

Similar theoretical developments have been apparent in research on unpaid care. For while there has been a long standing reluctance to engage with issues of culture within welfare systems (Baldock, 1999) and a corresponding avoidance of the long discredited 'cultural determinism' apparent in some first generation perspectives (Lewis, 1998), this trend has more recently been countered (Twigg & Martin, 2015). Thus some commentators on unpaid care suggest the need for a greater recognition of cultural and attitudinal factors that can mediate between carers and service receipt. These include the attitude that carers adopt towards their caring role, their gender, age, class and race and the views of the cared for person and other kin (Purkis & Ceci, 2015). In accordance with this, Chamberlayne and King (2000), drawing on the biographies and strategies of carers in Britain and Germany, found that patterns of informal caring are not just direct products of official welfare systems but also arise from such things as the gender and generation of welfare subjects. These issues have been enlarged upon in the 'cultures of care' approach (Fine, 2015), which suggests that there should be more recognition of the complex interplay between formal and informal support within ageing societies with the availability of the latter, not necessarily reflecting the lack of availability of the former.

2.2.3   Looking Backwards and Moving Forwards

As previous sections have demonstrated, recent developments and the incorporation of different generations of thought have helped to counter the fragmentation that has long characterised research into both older age and unpaid care. However, in spite of these developments, many knowledge gaps remain. Thus with regard to unpaid care, not only has the diffuse and divided focus of research on this issue continued to overlook older spouse carers and older carers more generally, but it has also undermined a full understanding of the caring role. For it has tended to create a false dichotomy between the interests of carers and care receivers, overlooking their interdependence and their common need for support (O'Rourke et al., 2021). It has also regarded caregiving as isolatable from other aspects of life (Purkis & Ceci, 2015) and neglected the material, organisational and cultural worlds (Fine, 2015) that can influence unpaid caring and the 'social risk' that can arise from this role (Morgan, 2018)

Within the area of social gerontology, similar issues have been explored by Grenier et al. (2017) who maintain that due to the rejection by third generation approaches of the physical and social determinism of preceding generations, there has, henceforth, been an inadequate recognition of the way in which the fourth age of life is socially constructed. Thus, drawing on the concept of 'precarity', they attempt to shift the focus of debates on dependency in the fourth age towards a greater recognition of shared vulnerability and responsibilities for care. This is itself characterised by intersectionality along the lines of class, gender and other social divisions (Twigg & Martin, 2015). Similarly, with regard to concepts of embodiment (Tulle, 2015), the impact of ageing on the body is not simply a result of physical processes but is also socially structured due to such things as the influence of socio-economic factors on this impact (Twigg & Martin, 2015). Moreover, as Lloyd et al. (2014) observe, in spite of the focus of third generation approaches on action and meaning, there has been a relative lack of understanding of the perceptions of those experiencing bodily decline and the transition to dependency in the fourth age.

Even less is known, as yet, on the way in which unpaid carers and more specifically older spouse carers, perceive and manage the transition to frailty in their partners, and sometimes also in themselves and the optimum way in which service provision can respond to this. For if the fourth age of life is shaped and defined by institutional practices (Lloyd et al., 2014), then it would follow that such practices can also help to ameliorate its impact and promote positive meanings for this life stage. This would not only benefit older people themselves but would also help to overcome the cultural failure to fully engage with physical and mental decline in later life (Grenier et al., 2017; Lloyd et al., 2014). In order to address these omissions, there is a need for more research into the issue of unpaid caring and older age and a greater integration in the theoretical perspectives and approaches drawn upon. In view of the multiple influences on the lives of older spouse carers, this should incorporate consideration of activity, agency and choice on one hand and structure, constraint and context on the other, as well as the way in which these factors dynamically interplay over the later life course.

Similar integration is needed in the methods utilised in this research which should transcend longstanding methodological divides and take account of the dual nature of human experience. This need has been recognised by some researchers who are increasingly adopting a pragmatic rather than dogmatic approach to methodological choice and using a combination of complimentary methods (Larkin et al., 2019). Thus quantitative research can facilitate qualitative approaches by helping to uncover the generality of phenomena observed, as seen for example in the secondary analysis of statistics performed by Arber and Ginn (1993). On the other hand, as it will be seen in Chaps. 4, 5, 6, and 7, qualitative methods can 'look behind' statistical data and investigate the relationships between variables uncovered by this data. It will be the purpose of the next chapter to further pursue some of these themes and to explore the way in which, in spite of rhetoric towards responsive and culturally sensitive service provision, policy and practice have failed to recognise or respond to the needs of older spouse carers. This has been apparent both on a direct level through the lack of services available to meet their specific needs and on an indirect level through the provision of services that are incompatible with these needs.

REFERENCES

Andréasson, F., Mattsson, T., & Hanson, E. (2023). The balance in our relationship has changed: Everyday family living, couplehood and digital spaces in informal spousal care. *Journal of Family Studies, 29*(2), 719–737.

Arber, S., & Ginn, J. (1993). Class, caring and the life-course. In S. Arber & M. Evandrou (Eds.), *Ageing, independence and the life-course* (pp. 149–168). Jessica Kingsley.

Baldock, J. (1999). Culture: The missing variable in understanding social policy? *Social Policy and Administration, 33*(4), 458–473.

Beresford, P. (2002). User involvement in research and evaluation: Liberation or regulation? *Social Policy and Society, 1*(2), 95–105.

Carers Trust. (2015). *Caring about older carers: Providing support for people caring in later life.* Carers Trust.

Carers UK. (2022). *State of caring 2022: A snapshot of unpaid care in the UK.* Carers UK.

Chamberlayne, P., & King, A. (2000). *Cultures of care: Biographies of carers in Britain and the two Germanies.* Policy Press.

Colombo, F., Llena-Nozal, A., Mercier, J., & Tjadens, F. (2011). *Help wanted?* OECD Health Policy Studies, OECD Publishing.

Cooper, B., & Harrop, A. (2023). *Support guaranteed: The roadmap to a national care service.* Fabian Society.

Cumming, E., & Henry, W. (1962). *Growing old: The process of disengagement.* Basic Books.

Eurocarers. (2023). Retrieved December 1, 2023, from https://eurocarers.org

Fetherstonhaugh, D., Rayner, J., & Tarzia, L. (2019). Hanging on to some autonomy in decision making: How do spouse carers support this. *Dementia, 18*(4), 1219–1236.

Finch, J., & Groves, D. (Eds.). (1983). *A Labour of Love: Women, work and caring.* Routledge and Kegan Paul.

Fine, M. (2015). Cultures of care. In J. Twigg & W. Martin (Eds.), *Routledge handbook of cultural gerontology* (pp. 269–276). Routledge.

Gilleard, C., & Higgs, P. (2000). *Cultures of ageing: Self, citizen and the body.* Prentice Hall.

Gilleard, C., & Higgs, P. (2010). Aging without agency: Theorising the fourth age. *Aging and Mental Health, 14*(2), 121–128.

Grad, J., & Sainsbury, P. (1968). The effects that patients have on their families. *British Journal of Psychiatry, 114*, 265–278.

Greenwood, N., & Smith, R. (2016). The oldest carers: A narrative review and synthesis of the experiences of carers aged over 75 years. *Maturitas, 94*, 161–172.

Grenier, A., Lloyd, L., & Phillipson, C. (2017). Precarity in late life: Rethinking dementia as a 'frailed' old age. *Sociology of Health & Illness, 39*(2), 318–330.

Harper, S. (2010). The capacity of social security and health care institutions to adapt to an ageing world. *International Social Security Review, 63*(3–4), 177–196.

International Alliance of Carer Organisations. (2021). *Global state of caring.* Retrieved May 24, 2023, from IACO-Global-State-of-Caring-July-13.pdf (internationalcarers.org).

International Labour Organisation. (2018). *Care work and care jobs for the future of decent work.* International Labour Office.

Johansson, M., McKee, K., Dahlberg, L., Summer Meranius, M., Williams, C., & Marmstål Hammar, L. (2022). Negative impact and positive value of caregiving in spouse carers of persons with dementia in Sweden. *International Journal of Environmental Research and Public Health, 19*(3), 1788.

Larkin, M. (2017). Supporting caring and carers in later life. *Innovation in Aging, 1*(1), 1109.

Larkin, M., Henwood, M., & Milne, A. (2019). Carer related research and knowledge: Findings from a scoping review. *Health and Social Care in the Community, 27*(1), 55–67.

Larkin, M., Henwood, M., & Milne, A. (2022). Older carers and carers of people with dementia: Improving and developing effective support. *Social Policy and Society, 21*(2), 242–256.

Lewis, O. (1998). The culture of poverty. *Society, 35*(2), 7–9.

Lloyd, L., Calnan, M., Cameron, A., Seymour, J., & Smith, R. (2014). Identity in the fourth age: Perseverance, adaptation and maintaining dignity. *Ageing and Society, 34*(1), 1–19.

Milligan, C. (2005). From home to 'home': Situating emotions within the caregiving experience. *Environment and Planning A, 37*(12), 2105–2120.

Morgan, F. (2018). The treatment of informal care-related risks as social risks: An analysis of the English care policy system. *Journal of Social Policy, 47*(1), 179–196.

Morgan, T., Bharmal, A., Duschinsky, R., & Barclay, S. (2020). Experiences of oldest-old caregivers whose partner is approaching end-of-life: A mixed-method systematic review and narrative synthesis. *PLoS One, 15*(6), e0232401.

Morris, J. (1993). *Independent lives: Community care and disabled people.* Macmillan.

Murray, J., Schneider, J., Banerjee, S., & Mann, A. (1999). Eurocare: A cross-national study of co-resident spouse carers for people with Alzheimer's Disease. *International Journal of Geriatric Psychiatry, 14*, 662–667.

O'Rourke, G., Lloyd, L., Bezzina, A., Cameron, A., Jessiman, T., & Smith, R. (2021). Supporting older co-resident carers of older people – The impact of care act implementation in four local authorities in England. *Social Policy and Society, 20*(3), 371–384.

Office for National Statistics. (2023a). Census 2021 Statistics, *Unpaid care by age sex and deprivation in England and Wales,* Published 13 February, 2023.

Office for National Statistics. (2023b). Census 2021 statistics. *Disability by age, sex and deprivation in England and Wales,* Published 8 February, 2023.

Office for National Statistics. (2023c). Census 2021 statistics. *Profile of the older population living in England and Wales in 2021 and changes since 2011,* Published 3 April, 2023.

Ornstein, K., Wolff, J., Bollens-Lund, E., Rahman, O. K., & Kelley, A. (2019). Spousal caregivers are caregiving alone in the last years of life. *Health Affairs, 38*(6), 964–972.

Parker, G. (1993). *With this body: Caring and disability in marriage.* Open University Press.

Parker, R. (1981). *Tending and social policy.* Policy Studies Institute.

Phillipson, C. (1982). *Capitalism and the construction of old age.* Macmillan.

Phillipson, C. (2013). *Ageing.* John Wiley and Sons.

Purkis, M., & Ceci, C. (2015). Problematizing care burden research. *Ageing and Society, 35*(7), 1410–1428.

Qureshi, H., & Walker, A. (1989). *The caring relationship.* Macmillan.

Tanner, D. (2010). *Managing the ageing experience: Learning from older people.* Policy Press.

Tulle, E. (2015). Theorising embodiment and ageing. In J. Twigg & W. Martin (Eds.), *Routledge handbook of cultural gerontology* (pp. 125–132). Routledge.

Turjamaa, R., Salpakari, J., & Koskinen, L. (2020). Experiences of older spousal caregivers for caring a person with a memory disorder. *Healthcare, 8*(2), 95.

Twigg, J., & Atkin, K. (1994). *Carers perceived*. Open University Press.

Twigg, J., & Martin, W. (Eds.). (2015). *Routledge handbook of cultural gerontology*. Routledge.

Wilding, P. (2018). The evolution of social welfare. In P. Bean & S. MacPherson (Eds.), *Approaches to welfare*. Routledge.

CHAPTER 3

Entering the World of Older Spouse Carers

Abstract In addition to the important impact of demographic trends and contextual factors such as socio-economic status on the incidence of care between older spouses, developments in policy and practice have also had a significant impact on this incidence. These developments and their implications for older spouse carers and unpaid carers more generally will be explored in the first part of this chapter. The second part will give details of the author's own research into older spouse carers, the findings of which will be drawn upon in subsequent chapters.

Keywords Welfare partnership • Welfare pluralism • Community care • Neo-liberal • Welfare exclusion • Method

As seen in Chap. 2, demographic trends towards an ageing population have potentially led to increasing demands on unpaid care provision (Cooper & Harrop, 2023; Morgan et al., 2020). Due to the fact that this care is an 'integrated' activity, potentially transcending the boundary between private and public domains (Tronto, 1993), policy and practice trends have had a similar impact. Thus, as a result of deinstitutionalisation, community care policies and cuts to public services, recent decades have seen an increased emphasis placed on unpaid care with most people in need of long term care now receiving this care at home (Cooper & Harrop, 2023). The first part of this chapter will further explore these developments in policy and practice and their implications for older spouse carers. This will be followed by an introduction to the authors own research into the experiences of these carers which will be drawn upon throughout the book.

3.1   POLICY AND PRACTICE TRENDS

3.1.1   A Changing Welfare Partnership

Recent years have seen a shifting dynamic within the welfare partnership between the family and the state and a transition from care in to care by the community with an ever increasing emphasis being placed on informal sources of support (Cooper & Harrop, 2023). In accordance with this, public health systems around the world have pursued community solutions to care provision and laws mandating the unpaid care of dependent relatives (International Alliance of Carer Organisations, 2021). For example, in the 1990s the emphasis in German social assistance law was transferred from care in institutions to community-based care while the European Union has supported care in community projects through the European Social Fund (Larkin, 2017). Accompanying the increasing emphasis on the role of unpaid carers in welfare provision, there has been a changing approach towards their needs. According to Twigg and Atkin (1994), during the welfare consensus this approach was guided by a 'carers as resources' model with provision being largely aimed at the care recipient in order to promote their independence and subsequent reliance on informal sources of support. They maintain that this has subsequently been replaced by the 'carers as co-client' model which recognises that carers have needs in their own right which may conflict with those of the care recipient (Twigg & Atkin, 1994). This issue has been elaborated by Tronto (1993) who offers an 'ideal type' model of care and identifies both carers and care receivers as active agents in its practice.

This changing approach to carers has been reflected in subsequent research which, as it was shown in the previous chapter, has taken an increasing interest in the diverse experiences and support needs of unpaid carers (Larkin et al., 2019). It has also been reflected in policy and practice developments which are increasingly aimed at unpaid carers and which recognises their potentially independent needs as co-clients (O'Rourke et al., 2021). Within the UK, relevant measures have included the introduction of benefits such as the Carers Allowance for full time unpaid carers as well as Attendance Allowance for those in need of care. Other developments include the NHS and Community Care Act 1990 which requires that social work assessments should not only be needs led but should also take account of the interests of the carer as well as those of the client. This requirement has been further formalised by the Carers Act 1995 which places a legal obligation on local authorities to assess the ability of carers to provide and continue to provide care. This has been consolidated by the Care Act 2014 which sets out in one place, local authorities' duties in relation to assessing carers needs and their eligibility for publicly funded care and support, aiming to provide parity of esteem between those giving and receiving care (O'Rourke et al., 2021). In addition, recent years have seen the launching of a series of National Carers Strategies by the UK government and a White Paper on adult social care entitled 'People at the Heart of Care: Adult Social Care Reform' (Department of Health, 2021). This has further underlined the government's commitment to carers through the provision of extra funding and the expressed goal of improving the quality and availability of formal support provision.

These policy developments have been accompanied by the emergence of various organisations around the world which aim to support and represent unpaid carers and caring. For example, established in 2012, the International Alliance of Carer Organisations (2021) is a coalition of non-governmental carer organisations. It aims to identify and address common caregiver challenges with the goal of increasing awareness of the needs of caregivers and influencing policy, programs and services. In doing so it has identified six universal carer priorities including recognition, financial support, work and education, health and wellbeing, information and knowledge and evidence informed practices. While within Europe, Eurocarers (2023) brings together carers organisations, universities and research institutes with a view to promoting evidence based advocacy for unpaid carers. A similar organisational focus has been apparent in the UK which has seen the establishment of an All-Party Parliamentary Group which aims to better understand and represent the needs of unpaid carers. Also emerging are locally based carer support groups as well as organisations such as Carers UK and its international counterparts which aim to connect, campaign, help and innovate on behalf of carers (Carers UK, 2022).

Just as the increased focus on unpaid carers is indicative of a marginalisation of the role of the state in providing this care, a similar marginalisation of statutory responsibilities has become apparent with the emergence of a neo-liberal stance to welfare provision. This has aimed to create a dual system of care and a purchaser-provider split in which the state is a manager of care rather than a provider of it (Cooper & Harrop, 2023). Thus community care policy has become characterised by a system of welfare pluralism and a targeting and consumerisation of welfare provision, placing increasing emphasis on means testing and on non-statutory forms of support in favour of that provided by statutory sources. The stated aims of these developments have been to increase room for choice, encourage flexibility and stimulate innovation thus promoting services that are more sensitive to the needs and perspectives of individual welfare recipients (Argyle et al., 2017). These developments in welfare pluralism have been accompanied by a shift towards perspectives in welfare which reject the preceding principles of top down and universalistic welfare provision, which is regarded as being patronising and dependency creating. In its place, a bottom-up and personalised approach to assessment and intervention has been increasingly advocated with the expressed goal of promoting the individual service user as active consumers and enhancing their independence (Barnes, 2012).

3.1.2   Welfare Exclusion

Within the UK, the political rationale behind these combined developments can be seen as originating in the ideology of the new right and Thatcherism which maintained that the welfare state was expensive, over protective and bureaucratic. The solution was in pushing back the boundaries of the state in order to promote individual responsibility and family values. In spite of these stated aims, critics maintain that these developments are simply another means of managing increasing demand for limited resources through delay, diversion and exclusion (Cooper & Harrop, 2023) and marginalising many support services from the mainstream of adult social care provision (O'Rourke et al., 2021). Moreover, the emphasis placed by neo-liberal approaches to welfare policy and practice on the way in which carers subjectively define their situation rather than on the provision of practical help to change the objective reality of their life can not only be seen as the result of increasing resource constraint. It can also be seen as the result of the influence of postmodernism on welfare according to which there should be more focus on diversity and identity of service users rather than on the shared conditions of their existence (Twigg & Martin, 2015). However, in recognising the diversity of services users, neo-liberal approaches have obscured their commonality and their shared need for adequate, affordable and accessible support while also neglecting the contextual factors from which this diversity can arise (Purkis & Ceci, 2015). For example, although cuts in social care spending have been apparent throughout the UK, it is poorer communities that have felt their impact most keenly with the less well-off being much more likely than better off counterparts to be lacking in the support they need (Cooper & Harrop, 2023).

Not only is there a gap between the rhetoric and reality of recent developments in welfare provision, these developments have also given rise to underlying tensions and contradictions in the support provided (Morgan, 2018; O'Rourke et al., 2021). Thus, on one hand, policy rhetoric and intervention have recognised the burdens of unpaid carers and their potential conflict of interest with the cared for person. On the other hand, policy developments and progressive cuts to social care funding have potentially exacerbated these burdens (Cooper & Harrop, 2023). As Morgan (2018) observes, this is embodied in the concept of 'social risk' in the caring relationship which is increasingly being privatised to the individual rather than alleviated through social intervention due to inadequate and inconsistent welfare services (O'Rourke et al., 2021). While the corresponding emphasis on supporting carer resilience, self-help and independence has further ensured this 'privatisation' (Tronto, 1993) and the 'social risk' arising from it (Morgan, 2018). As such, within the UK, there is a growing social care funding gap with the number of adults in receipt of this care progressively falling in spite of trends towards an ageing population and with 2.6 million people in England aged over 50 having an unmet meet for support (Cooper & Harrop, 2023). Services specifically aimed at unpaid carers have also been under resourced with Carers UK (2022) in their survey of such carers, finding that only one in four had received a carer's assessment and that many of those who had received one said that it did not meet their needs. In addition, the fragmentation of the welfare system (Cooper & Harrop, 2023) can see many people finding themselves in 'no care zones' or 'falling through the gaps' due to poorly integrated services that can be difficult and confusing to access (Argyle et al., 2017; Grenier et al., 2021). The increased use of means testing and charging for these services is likely to have a similar impact (O'Rourke et al., 2021) with some carers being unable or unwilling to pay for such services or being unaware of what services are potentially available to them (Carers UK, 2022).

Although these developments in policy and practice have important implications for all unpaid carers and service users more generally, their impact is likely to be especially significant for older spouse carers (O'Rourke et al., 2021). This is partly due demographic trends towards and ageing population and the adapted 'intergenerational contract' arising from this with older people being increasingly expected to take responsibility for the care of themselves and their contemporaries (Harper, 2010). It is also due to the increasing targeting of services at the most vulnerable and at those who live alone which will disproportionately affect older spouse carers whose partner is likely to be highly dependent but may still be excluded from support (Argyle et al., 2017; Cooper & Harrop, 2023). This disadvantage is compounded by the common invisibility of older spouse carers within the welfare system due to assumptions about their role held by service providers as well as by many carers themselves (O'Rourke et al., 2021). Thus, it is common for spouse carers to regard their role as being a normal and natural part of the marital relationship and the mutual exchanges taking place within it, leading them to resist intrusion from outside agencies (Morgan et al., 2020).

In spite of these high levels of interdependence in the caring relationships of older spouse carers, there is very little support available to former carers to help them to adjust to the loss of their caring role and the practical and emotional problems that may arise from this (Larkin & Milne, 2017). This interdependence is further overlooked by individualised assessments which falsely construct two potentially conflicting subjects within caring relationships, overlooking the way in which needs may coincide within these relationships (Barnes, 2012). Linked with the high levels of interdependence within the spousal caring relationship are the high levels of stoicism found to be apparent in older spouse carers (Morgan et al., 2020) and older people more generally (Lloyd et al., 2014) which can form a further barrier to service access. For not only may they not identify as being a caregiver but they may also reject the need for such support and the sense of victimhood it may imply. Such attitudes can also run counter to a system that expects welfare recipients to be active consumers, shopping around for services and often means that such services are only accessed when a crisis point is reached (Argyle et al., 2017). Just as attitudinal factors in older age can run counter to recent developments in service provision, the nature of ill health and disability in later life may be similarly conflicting. Thus, pressure for bed space in hospitals and the subsequent rapid discharge of patients can have negative implications for older people as they may be incompatible with their tendency to take longer to recuperate than younger age groups. While the likelihood of older people to experience more than one chronic condition means that they often require attention from multiple service providers giving rise to particular difficulties in navigating their way around fragmented and poorly coordinated health and social care systems (OECD, 2020).

In addition to the indirect neglect of older spouse carers through services which tend to be inadequate or incompatible to their own or their partner's specific needs, a more obvious neglect is apparent in the paucity of interventions which aim to address these needs or those of older carers more generally. This contrasts with the profusion of international projects which are aimed at the specific needs of young carers with the Global State of Caring Report (International Alliance of Carer Organisations, 2021), showing that most of the 18 countries included in this report provided this targeted support to young carers. The report also reveals a great deal of focus amongst participating countries on the workplace issues faced by unpaid carers and a subsequent emphasis on practices which facilitate supportive work and educational environments for such carers. A similar emphasis is apparent in recent UK based policy recommendations which highlight the need for greater help to be given to unpaid carers to obtain and sustain paid employment (Cooper & Harrop, 2023). For example, The Carers Leave Act 2023 gives employees the right to unpaid leave in order to accommodate their caring responsibilities. Regardless of the merits of these measures, they obviously do not address the needs of older spouse carers who tend to be retired. While the fact that many forms of innovative practice aimed at carers involve the use of online groups or apps can also exclude many older and poorer carers with lack of internet access being a major barrier to involvement (Carers UK, 2022). Similar marginalisation is apparent in the benefits system with the UK Carers Allowance which is potentially available to those providing care on a full time basis being unavailable to those over state retirement age, regardless of the intensity of their caring role.

3.2   THE STUDY

3.2.1   Setting the Scene

As preceding discussions have illustrated, in spite of the growing interest in the issue of unpaid carers, the experiences and needs of older spouse carers have been largely neglected both in research and in policy and practice interventions (Morgan et al., 2020). Thus with regard to research, in spite of the many parallels in the evolution of literature on unpaid care on one hand and older age on the other, this literature has been characterised by a lack of integration leading to significant knowledge gaps. These gaps have been compounded by the fragmentation of approach and focus which has characterised research in both these areas, serving to undermine the insights provided (Purkis & Ceci, 2015; Twigg & Martin, 2015). Similar omissions have been apparent in welfare provision. For although the specific needs of certain groups of carers, such as young carers, have gained extensive recognition, interventions for older spouse carers have either been non-existent or been characterised by a generalised support model which is incompatible with their particular needs (Morgan et al., 2020). While in spite of the advocacy of cultural approaches to welfare, such approaches are hard to find, especially relating to older people, leaving many unanswered questions relating to this culture, particularly with regard to the unique experiences of older spouse carers (Morgan et al., 2020). With a view to redressing this neglect, this section will give details of the author's own research involving in depth interviews 26 older spouse carers, the findings of which will be drawn upon in subsequent chapters.

These interviews were conducted as part of a UK based ESRC funded study (Argyle, 2003) and were then revisited and reanalysed in subsequent research including a further ESRC funded study (Argyle & Warren, 2005) as well as in the process of writing this book. The benefits of reusing research data in this way is being increasingly recognised and is reflected in the emergence of a number of data archives such as Qualidata at the University of Essex (Bishop & Kuula-Luumi, 2017). Main benefits of this reuse are that it saves time and resources, maximises research visibility, minimises respondent burden, exposes data to new interpretations and allows for the pursuit of emerging themes (Hughes & Tarrant, 2019). As Hughes and Tarrant (2019) observe, these benefits are further enhanced if this reuse is performed by a researcher who is familiar with the initial study and its methods, methodological frameworks and context. As such, since the original carer interviews took place, the demographic and policy context of caring has evolved considerably leading to ever greater demands on their role (Cooper & Harrop, 2023; Morgan et al., 2020). As it has been seen in preceding discussions, combined with these developments have been the emergence of new perspectives and approaches both with regard to older age (Twigg & Martin, 2015) and to unpaid care (Larkin et al., 2019). These help to shed new light on the issues being addressed and allow for the further exploration of themes arising from the original data relating to the unique nature of the spousal caring relationship and the influence of material, attitudinal and physical issues on this relationship. These new perspectives and insights as well as relevant statistics will be drawn upon throughout the book.

3.2.2   Participant Recruitment

As it is never possible for qualitative research to include all relevant people in a given situation, sample selection is a necessary precondition to study commencement. For the purpose of this research, non-random sampling was felt to be preferable to the types of random sampling commonly used in quantitative research because such methods were inappropriate to the small scale of the study and its broadly exploratory aims (Hughes & Tarrant, 2019). Thus purposive sampling was widely used and involved the selection of participants conforming to the relevant criteria. As a precondition to sample selection, an appropriate source or sample frame had to be identified and access to it negotiated. One possible sample frame was the patient list of general practitioners (Qureshi & Walker, 1989). However, while such lists have been found to cover the vast majority of the local population, it would have been impossible to identify from these lists all of those involved in co-resident caring. Access to these lists would have also involved possibly lengthy negotiations with NHS ethics boards. As an alternative point of contact, local carer support groups were contacted with information about the research and an appeal for participants. However, only two carers were accessed through such sources (Mrs Lipset and Mrs Reid) and it was recognised that due to their tendency not to identify as carers (O'Rourke et al., 2021), many of those eligible would not be members of such groups. In view of these limitations, a number of statutory and voluntary agencies including home care services were approached with an appeal for participants, and it is from these sources that the majority of participants were eventually recruited.

In order to add a longitudinal dimension to the data (Hughes & Tarrant, 2019), follow-up interviews with participants were carried out where possible and, like the initial process of respondent recruitment, gaining access for these follow-up interviews was a relatively complex task. For, while all respondents had agreed to take part in a follow-up phase during their first interview, in attempting to contact these carers over a year after the initial interviews had taken place it was discovered that some of them were no longer contactable at their original addresses. Sometimes it was established that this was due to death or relocation, but in other cases, participants' whereabouts remained unclear, and due to the ethical sensitivities involved, it would not have felt appropriate to delve deeply into their whereabouts. As a result of this, only 9 of the original sample of 26 took part in the follow-up phase. This issue highlights an important problem in carrying out longitudinal research with older people, especially those at a later stage of the age spectrum and also demonstrates the considerable and ongoing transitions apparent in the lives of respondents. Nevertheless, when seen, all participants gave generously of their time, providing an invaluable insight into the 'world' of older spouse carers and without their contribution this book would not have been possible. Throughout the fieldwork, ethical principles of social research were applied and it was ensured that participants knew that their involvement was entirely voluntary and that they could opt out at any stage. Attention was also paid to the protection of the privacy and anonymity of respondents and it was ensured that their wellbeing was not adversely affected by their participation (Hughes & Tarrant, 2019). In accordance with this, all respondents were allocated a pseudonym, and principles of informed consent were also adhered to with the aims of the study being made clear to potential participants.

3.2.3   *Participant Profile*

All 26 participants were caring for partners with various impairments, most commonly this was dementia or an undiagnosed cognitive impairment with 6 spouses having a dementia diagnosis and with several others experiencing varying levels of confusion. A further 6 spouses were stroke survivors while the rest had various other mental and physical impairments and co-morbidities. Respondents had been caring for an average of about 10 years and this duration ranged widely from 1 to 36 years. In the interests of consistency, all were retired and co-resident with their spouse in two person households. They were made up of equal numbers of men and women, thus reflecting the broadly equal gender balance of caring in older age (Office for National Statistics, 2022). Their housing status was divided between 10 owner occupiers and 16 who rented their housing either privately or through the social rented sector. Their ages ranged between 68 and 92 with an average age of 80 and with the vast majority (20) being aged 75 and over. This inclusion of the 'older old' within the participating carers helps to redress the neglect of this group which is apparent in much research into older carers and unpaid carers more generally (Morgan et al., 2020). For as Morgan et al. (2020) observe, the particular issues faced by older spouse carers are likely to be magnified amongst carers aged over 75. These include the accelerated and often mutual onset of disability and dependency within the caring relationship and the greater caring demands experienced as a result of this as well as such things as declining social networks and the meanings and strategies adopted towards the caring role.

Respondents were characterised by a certain degree of diversity along the lines of age, disability, gender and housing status. However, all were living within heterosexual relationships and most were white and British with only two respondents, Mr Cicourel, a white Italian and Mr Denis, a black Jamaican, originating from backgrounds outside the UK, both having moved to England in their twenties in pursuit of work. Moreover, while in most cases, only one partner in each spousal relationship has been identified as a carer in this study, this has not been the case for two couples, Mr and Mrs Taylor and Mrs and Mrs Lane. For these couples were apparently involved in wholly interdependent caring relationships in which it was impossible to distinguish between the care giver and care receiver. All four of these spouses have therefore been categorised as carers. The main details of participants are shown in Table 3.1 and are described in more detail throughout subsequent chapters.

All respondents lived in a city in England. According to official statistics, at the time the interviews were carried out, 10.91 per cent of city residents performed an unpaid caring role, this compares to 10 per cent of the city population in more recent census data (Office for National Statistics, 2001, 2022). However while the total percentage of unpaid carers has slightly fallen since 2001, the percentage of carers performing a high intensity role has risen (2022 percentages shown in brackets).

19 hours a week or less for 7.15 per cent of residents in 2001 (4.7 per cent in 2022)

20 to 49 hours a week for 1.27 per cent of residents in 2001 (2.1 per cent in 2022)

50 or more hours a week for 2.49 per cent of residents in 2001 (3.2 per cent in 2022)

In spite of these changes over time in the incidence of high-intensity caring, a consistent feature of this incidence has been its uneven distribution throughout the city which is linked to the corresponding incidence of

Table 3.1 Participant profile

Name	Age	Impairment of spouse	Years caring	Car owner	Housing status
Mrs Flude	68	Dementia	6	Yes	Owner
Mrs Reid	68	Anxiety and depression	4	No	Tenant
Mr Cicourel	69	Multiple sclerosis	20	Yes	Owner
Mrs Lipset	69	Dementia	36	No	Owner
Mrs Harris	70	Stroke	3	No	Tenant
Mrs Gibbons	73	Stroke	2	Yes	Owner
Mrs Bell	75	Dementia	1	No	Tenant
Mr Carson	78	Dementia	2	No	Tenant
Mr Hall	78	Anxiety and depression	20	No	Tenant
Mr Hart	78	Stroke	2	No	Tenant
Mr MacLellan	78	Parkinson's disease	20	Yes	Tenant
Mrs Phillips	79	Emphysema	2	No	Tenant
Mrs Williams	79	Stroke	4	No	Tenant
Mrs Field	82	Dementia	10	Yes	Owner
Mrs Roach	84	Kidney disease and confusion	25	No	Owner
Mrs Taylor	84	Heart and sight problems	13	No	Tenant
Mr Tumin	84	Stroke and confusion	3	No	Tenant
Mr Denis	85	Stroke and confusion	10	No	Tenant
Mr Wilson	85	Multiple physical impairments	22	No	Tenant
Mr Lane	86	Heart and mobility problems	5	No	Owner
Mrs Lane	86	Mobility impairment	2	No	Owner
Mr Caplow	87	Diverticulitis and heart problems	12	No	Tenant
Mrs Coates	88	Heart and mobility problems	10	No	Owner
Mr Hunter	89	Dementia	1	Yes	Owner
Mr Tunstall	91	Mobility and sight impairments	20	No	Tenant
Mr Taylor	92	Heart and sight problems	13	No	Tenant

ill health, disability and deprivation. Thus, low intensity caring for 19 hours a week or less is most commonly found in areas with high proportions of older residents. Conversely, medium and high intensity caring for 20 hours or more is more strongly associated, not with age profiles, but with the incidence of poor health and high levels of deprivation which tend to be concentrated in the North and South East of the city (Office for National Statistics, 2001, 2022). As such, while in many respects it is a relatively average city with average overall levels of mortality and deprivation, it is also a city of extremes with patterns of deprivation being unevenly spread. Thus around a third of its neighbourhoods are amongst the most deprived in the country while around a quarter of neighbourhoods are amongst the most affluent. In contrast to other cities, these extremes in deprivation are not separated by great distances and significant social and economic polarity is contained within a relatively small area. These extremes have important implications for carers suggesting that welfare services within the city recognise and respond to the needs of a carer population whose circumstances and life experiences are very diverse.

3.2.4   Data Collection and Analysis

Semi-structured interviews were conducted with the 26 older spouse carers recruited to the study. These interviews were between one and four hours in duration and took place in the carers own home. They were asked a series of open ended and exploratory questions about their lives as well as some closed ended questions eliciting personal details including their age, ethnicity and living arrangements. In order to avoid 'reinventing the wheel' and to fully utilise existing expertise, questions were constructed with reference to many indicators utilised in previous relevant research. For example, as one of the aims of the research was to redress the neglect of socio-economic issues apparent in much research into unpaid care, carers were questioned on their housing status. As other research has noted (Age UK, 2022), this measure was felt to be preferable to the occupational categories commonly used to determine such status for three main reasons. Firstly, in retirement the significance of occupational status is likely to be diminished while housing will continue to have a daily impact on the lives of respondents. Secondly, information on housing status is easy to elicit and relatively unambiguous in comparison to attempting to ascertain occupational status, especially for older women some of whom have rarely been in paid employment. Thirdly, within the UK, there is a strong correlation between housing status and socio-economic status more generally (Age UK, 2022) with housing status becoming a key social divide overriding all other social and occupational divisions. Thus in their recent survey, Age UK (2022) found that the oldest old and those who rent their home are at particular risk of poverty with 38 per cent of private tenants and 36 per cent of social rented sector tenants, living in poverty compared to 14 per cent of older people who are home owners.

In addition, questions on the impact of caring were adapted from existing research on the issue and the areas of life identified in this research including household routine, mental and physical health, social life and finances (Grad & Sainsbury, 1968; Larkin et al., 2019). However, these questions were not adopted uncritically and in contrast to much early research on the impact of caring (Grad & Sainsbury, 1968; Purkis & Ceci, 2015), carers were able to give positive as well as negative responses when questioned about this impact. This adaptation helped to avoid the marginalisation of respondent's perspectives and this was further facilitated by the inclusion of open ended questions. The exploratory nature of these open ended questions combined with a reflexive approach to questionnaire design enabled the identification of emergent issues to be pursued in subsequent interviews (Glaser & Strauss, 2017). For example, although not incorporated into the original questionnaire, the issue of car ownership and access to transport more generally quickly emerged as an important influence of the lives of respondents, and questions incorporating this issue were therefore incorporated into interviews. Just as questions were adapted in the light of carer responses, so was their administration. Thus it was originally intended that, rather than incorporating all of the questions in one interview, some would be administered through a short questionnaire. The rationale behind this decision was that carers would find it easier to disclose sensitive issues through a relatively impersonal format. However, contrary to these expectations, all of the carers preferred to be 'talked through' the questions rather than completing them alone as it allowed them to clarify their thoughts and feelings and also enabled the interviewer to reflect back on what they had previously said, if they were in any doubt on how to respond.

Not only did this process of adaptation help to ensure that respondents perceptions had some influence on research design, it also helped to promote the validity of the data produced by minimising its distortion and by avoiding the imposition of preconceived and inflexible categories (Glaser & Strauss, 2017). Such validity can also be promoted by enhancing the scope and depth of research through the use of methodological triangulation which helps to transcend the limited potential of the individual method (Larkin et al., 2019). One way in which this depth and scope was added to this study was through the use, where possible, of follow-up interviews which allowed an exploration of the way in which the carer's life had changed since the initial interviews. This process was further facilitated by the inclusion within the follow-up interviews of an exploration of the biography of the respondent which helped to show how events unfolded and interrelated over the life course. Another benefit of follow-up interviews were that they allowed for the pursuit of themes emerging from initial interviews and the provision of feedback on these themes. These themes were further enhanced and highlighted (Hughes, 1998) through the production of carer vignettes.

In accordance with the principles of grounded theory (Glaser & Strauss, 2017), a flexible and iterative approach was taken not only to the collection of data but also in its subsequent analysis. This analysis involved the use of the 'constant comparative method' (Glaser & Strauss, 2017) and which allows theoretical and conceptual elaboration to emerge on an ongoing basis. A necessary precondition to this constant comparative method was the use of coding with interview data being broken down into component parts. Analytical memos were also used with themes emerging from interviews being recorded in a series of such memos, which assisted in the analysis of data as well as in organising findings. However, as it was shown in Chap. 2, in spite of the merits of qualitative research, its focus on individual meaning and motives can overlook the way in which these are constrained by objective social forms and the systematic differences that can arise from this (Larkin et al., 2019). In the light of this and in order to provide an international perspective qualitative findings have been supplemented by reviews of existing literature and by relevant official statistics on unpaid caring and older age. These include the latest statistics from decennial UK Census (Office for National Statistics, 2022) as well as data from other national and international organisations such as Carers UK (2022), Age UK (2022), the International Alliance of Carer Organisations (2021) and the Organisation for Economic Cooperation and Development (OECD, 2020). It will be the purpose of the forthcoming chapters to present the findings of this research with the aim of illustrating and elaborating upon issues that have already been discussed.

References

Age UK. (2022). *Poverty in later life*. Age UK.

Argyle, E. (2003). *Caring and resources in older age*. PhD thesis, University of Sheffield. Retrieved May 24, 2023, from https://etheses.whiterose. ac.uk/5445/

Argyle, E., Kelly, T., Gladman, J., & Jones, R. (2017). The effective ingredients of social support at home for people with dementia: A literature review. *Journal of Integrated Care, 25*(2), 110–119.

Argyle, E., & Warren, L. (2005). *Older people and their money: Issues for policy and participation*, Cash and Care Conference, University of York. Retrieved May 24, 2023, from https://doi.org/10.13140/RG.2.2.13295.23209

Barnes, M. (2012). *Care in everyday life: An ethic of care in practice.* The Policy Press.

Bishop, L., & Kuula-Luumi, A. (2017). Revisiting qualitative data reuse: A decade on. *SAGE Open, 7*(1), 2158244016685136.

Carers, UK. (2022). *State of caring 2022: A snapshot of unpaid care in the UK.* Carers UK.

Cooper, B., & Harrop, A. (2023). *Support guaranteed: The roadmap to a national care service.* Fabian Society.

Department of Health. (2021). *People at the heart of care: adult social care reform.* HMSO.

Eurocarers. (2023). Retrieved December 1, 2023, from https://eurocarers.org

Glaser, B., & Strauss, A. (2017). *The discovery of grounded theory: Strategies for qualitative research.* Routledge.

Grad, J., & Sainsbury, P. (1968). The effects that patients have on their families. *British Journal of Psychiatry, 114*, 265–278.

Grenier, A., Phillipson, C., & Settersten, A. (Eds.). (2021). *Precarity and ageing: Understanding insecurity and risk in later life.* Policy Press.

Harper, S. (2010). The capacity of social security and health care institutions to adapt to an ageing world. *International Social Security Review, 63*(3–4), 177–196.

Hughes, K., & Tarrant, A. (Eds.). (2019). *Qualitative secondary analysis.* Sage.

Hughes, R. (1998). Considering the Vignette Technique and its application. *Sociology of Health and Illness, 20*(3), 381–400.

International Alliance of Carer Organisations. (2021). *Global state of caring.* Retrieved May 24, 2023, from IACO-Global-State-of-Caring-July-13.pdf (internationalcarers.org)

Larkin, M. (2017). Supporting caring and carers in later life. *Innovation in Aging, 1*(1), 1109.

Larkin, M., Henwood, M., & Milne, A. (2019). Carer related research and knowledge: Findings from a scoping review. *Health and Social Care in the Community, 27*(1), 55–67.

Larkin, M., & Milne, A. (2017). What do we know about older former carers? Key issues and themes. *Health and Social Care in the Community, 25*(4), 396–1403.

Lloyd, L., Calnan, M., Cameron, A., Seymour, J., & Smith, R. (2014). Identity in the fourth age: Perseverance, adaptation and maintaining dignity. *Ageing and Society, 34*(1), 1–19.

Morgan, F. (2018). The treatment of informal care-related risks as social risks: An analysis of the English care policy system. *Journal of Social Policy, 47*(1), 179–196.

Morgan, T., Bharmal, A., Duschinsky, R., & Barclay, S. (2020). Experiences of oldest-old caregivers whose partner is approaching end-of-life: A mixed-method systematic review and narrative synthesis. *PLoS One, 15*(6), e0232401.

O'Rourke, G., Lloyd, L., Bezzina, A., Cameron, A., Jessiman, T., & Smith, R. (2021). Supporting older co-resident carers of older people – The impact of care act implementation in four local authorities in England. *Social Policy and Society, 20*(3), 371–384.

OECD. (2020). *Who cares? Attracting and retaining care workers for the elderly.* OECD Health Policy Studies, Paris, OECD Publishing.

Office for National Statistics. (2001). Census 2001 statistics. *First results from Census 2001 in England and Wales,* Published June 2001.

Office for National Statistics. (2022). Census 2021 statistics. *First results from Census 2021 in England and Wales,* Published 28 June 2022.

Purkis, M., & Ceci, C. (2015). Problematizing care burden research. *Ageing and Society, 35*(7), 1410–1428.

Qureshi, H., & Walker, A. (1989). *The caring relationship.* Macmillan.

Tronto, J. (1993). *Moral boundaries: A Political argument for an ethic of care.* Routledge.

Twigg, J., & Atkin, K. (1994). *Carers perceived.* Open University Press.

Twigg, J., & Martin, W. (Eds.). (2015). *Routledge handbook of cultural gerontology.* Routledge.

CHAPTER 4

The Experiences of Older Spouse Carers

Abstract In order to redress the neglect of the experiences of older spouse carers, this chapter will be devoted to the exploration of these experiences from the perspectives of carers themselves. It will begin with a consideration of their views on the impact of caring upon their lives. This will draw on similar categories used in other carer research including the impact of caring on finances, health and social life. This will be followed by a consideration of the positive, negative and nuanced aspects of their caring experiences.

Keywords Carer burden • Carer experience • Caring role • Interdependence • Fourth age • Embodiment

In detailing the caring experiences of older spouse carers, this chapter will demonstrate that, contrary to traditional perceptions of older people as being the passive recipients of care, they are also the active providers of it and potentially perform demanding caring roles with implications for their own wellbeing (Morgan et al., 2020). Thus older spouse carers tend to be involved in caring for significant lengths of time with little respite. They are also more likely than younger counterparts to perform personal care activities such as washing and dressing which is, in its self, an indication of a 'high' level of caring involvement. However, the way in which this role is perceived by carers themselves can be nuanced and usually incorporates both positive and negative elements (Johansson et al., 2022).

4.1   IMPACTS

While the role of older spouse carers has been generally neglected, in spite of their significant demands, the experience of unpaid caring more generally has been very well addressed in a large number of research studies (Larkin et al., 2019). The focus of this research has tended to be divided with many studies attempting to objectively measure the burden or cost of this caring and its potentially negative impact on various aspects of carers lives (Purkis & Ceci, 2015). This impact of caring will be explored throughout this section.

4.1.1   Finances

Much research has identified the financial hardship experienced by carers. Thus on their annual survey of carers, Carers UK (2022) found that 63 percent of carers are 'extremely' worried about managing their monthly costs and that 25 percent of all carers are cutting back on essentials such as food and heating, a proportion that has nearly doubled since the previous year. This strong link between caring and poverty can be partially attributed to the reduced ability of carers to take on paid work. While this issue tends not to be relevant to older spouse carers as they are usually retired, long-term caring responsibilities could have a negative impact on their current pensions. For example, Mr Cicourel and Mr MacLellan had both taken early retirement in order to accommodate their caring responsibilities. In addition to the loss of income potentially arising from caring are the extra costs incurred by carers as a result of their partners disability. These costs include such things as paying for laundry, heating, transport, special food, housing, home adaptations and aids to mobility and daily living (Carers UK, 2022). Respondents in this sample spent large sums of money on such items:

> I had to have a stair lift fitted, we had to pay for it ourselves…and then I couldn't get in the car. Colin bought a newer car and he got a bigger one with higher seats so I can get in and when we go out he has a platform to help me get in and out. (Mrs Lane)

A source of recurrent expense for respondents was in the payment of charges for services such as home care and day care which are increasingly being incurred as a result of the consumerisation of welfare provision (Cooper & Harrop, 2023). Thus Mr Tumin described how, out of his weekly household income, he had to pay the running costs for his stair lift, home care bills, regular respite care bills and the rental of his 'lifeline' phone. However, perhaps surprisingly, some carers thought that their financial situation had actually improved as a result of caring. For some this was due to the receipt of welfare benefits such as Attendance Allowance. It could also be due to the fact that co-resident caring enabled the pooling of limited household resources.

4.1.2   *Physical Health*

Another major potential cost incurred as a result of caring is its impact upon the physical health of carers with Carers UK (2022) finding that 21 per cent of all unpaid carers surveyed said that their physical health was 'bad' or 'very bad'. Indeed many respondents in this sample spoke of health problems such as angina and arthritis and their impact on their caring role:

> When he first went into hospital I was younger but these last two years I started to feel my age. I'm 84 next Tuesday so I can't grumble. But I can't do what I want to do and that's what's upsetting me. (Mrs Roach)

The impairments of the cared for person could also have an important impact on the physical health of the carer, serving to exacerbate the demands of their role, as Mr MacLellan observed:

> It has got worse this last 12 months since she did her shoulder. She broke that just to be awkward and they didn't do a marvellous job on it. Well you can see. She can't use it sometimes, she can't feed herself. She's struggling but we've been coping anyway. With the continual lifting it's difficult, it's painful. (Mr MacLellan)

In spite of the physical health problems experienced by respondents, few maintained that these had been solely caused by caring with most carers seeing them as an inevitable product of the ageing process:

> I wouldn't say the wife has caused it. It's age catching up and I get breath-less when I'm walking and if I walk downstairs my knees start to give way. I can walk up steps better than I can walk down them. (Mr Tunstall)

As such, while this issue has often been neglected within gerontological research, it is undoubtedly the case that older people are more susceptible to health problems than younger age groups. This is upheld by statistics which show that around half of those aged 65 and over experience long term health problems or disabilities compared to around 1 in 10 of those aged under 65 (Office for National Statistics, 2022). This in turn is likely to increase the incidence of care between older spouses and increase the demands of this care due to the commonly progressive nature of decline in later life. With regard to this, Morgan et al. (2020) refer to the 'embodied impact' of such care and the 'double jeopardy' experienced by older spouse carers when this caring is combined with managing their own health problems (Morgan et al., 2020).

4.1.3   Mental Health

Although evidence on the role of unpaid caring in causing physical inca-pacity is relatively inconclusive, the relationship between such caring and mental health is much more evident. The strong link between caring and mental ill health has been upheld by much research which has found that such problems are more common in carers than in non-carers, especially when high intensity caring is involved (Twigg & Atkin, 1994). As such, the incidence of stress and depression amongst unpaid carers is widely recognised with Carers UK (2022) finding that 30 percent of carers expe-rienced 'bad' or 'very bad' mental health and with 60 percent of carers being worried about becoming stressed or anxious (Carers UK, 2022). In accordance with these findings several respondents in this research reported the negative impact of caring on their mental health:

> I think that caring does take a toll on you because you tend to get tired and then you get stressed and worried. (Mrs Reid)

Although the issue of abuse was not directly addressed in interviews with carers, such mental stresses are strongly associated with the incidence of this abuse which can be a two way process, particularly within the spou-sal relationship (Twigg & Martin, 2015).

Sometimes it gets you down doesn't it, I mean I lose my temper, I'll admit. (Mr MacLellan)

For many carers their mental strain was exacerbated by the behavioural problems of their spouse, especially those who had dementia or other forms of cognitive impairment:

It wears me down naturally. It's alright in the day time but at night time she'll have me out of bed anything up to six or seven times. It's the night time that punishes. I don't physically suffer, no, only tiredness if you can call that physical. (Mr Tumin)

4.1.4   Social Life

Associated with the stress arising from behavioural problems and the more general demands of caring is the further problem of 'restrictedness', that is, the feelings of boredom, claustrophobia and loneliness arising from the constraints that accompany the unpaid caring role (Twigg & Atkin, 1994). In accordance with this, Carers UK (2022) found that 33 per cent of those caring for more than 35 hours a week said that they felt lonely and 51 per cent said that taking a break would make them feel less lonely. These findings were reflected by respondents in this research. For example, Mr Cicourel spoke of his frustration at the time limits placed on his leisure activities due to his need to get back home to his wife:

I might have a week when she won't eat and she won't drink or it might take twenty minutes to give her a drink. So I can't commit myself to saying I'll be there at half past nine or ten o clock and because of that I think I'm making myself a nuisance and that's why I don't bother. (Mr Cicourel)

As Twigg and Atkin (1994) observe, this restrictedness takes three major forms. Firstly it arises from the carers need to ensure the care recipients physical safety, with this problem being reported by several respondents:

I can't leave her on her own; twice she's fallen down when I've just gone in the kitchen to make the tea. (Mr Hunter)

Secondly, it arises from the general anxiety of the carer about what might happen in their absence:

> I can't leave him. For one thing he gets very frightened, I think if he doesn't think I'm there. (Mrs Field)

A third aspect of restrictedness is 'secondary restrictedness'. That is, the carer may be reluctant to pursue an independent life without the cared for person. This secondary restrictedness is particularly apparent amongst spouse carers who may feel guilty about enjoying themselves without their partner and who, in contrast to non- spouse carers, are less likely to have developed an independent life prior to the onset of caring (Twigg & Atkin, 1994):

> Freedom is nice if you can share it. (Mr Cicourel)

In accordance with this, while respondents often maintained that their social life had got worse, they often said that they didn't mind as they didn't want to go out without their spouse:

> Even if I had someone to sit with her I wouldn't know where to go on my own. I wouldn't want to go in town and things like that. (Mr MacLellan)

In this respect, the perceived legitimacy of the independent activity was of great importance to spouse carers with such things as shopping being regarded as preferable to more frivolous social activities:

> I can leave her for an hour to go shopping which I have to do, I don't have any option. (Mr Tumin)

> Well I don't leave her long do I? If I dash to the shops and dash back, I leave her for half an hour at the most. (Mr McLellan)

While the often negative impacts of caring were faced to varying degrees by all respondents, as the case of Mr Carson helps to highlight (Vignette 4.1), the demands of caring for an older person with dementia have been found to be particularly diverse and complex.

Vignette 4.1: The Dementia Carer

The progressively changing demands of being an older spouse carer are well illustrated by the case of Mr Carson who was 78 and had looked after his 77 year old wife since she was diagnosed with dementia two years previously:

> If it had happened sooner it would have been harder but I retired at 62 which gave me quite a few years to gradually come in. (Mr Carson)

He did not feel that he had any great problem in adapting to his caring role as he said that it had been a gradual process of taking over housework tasks following his retirement:

> She did all the housework, only when I retired I used to help around the house a bit but now she can't do a thing, if she washes the pots, I have to watch her, I have to do everything. (Mr Carson)

However, as with many dementia carers, the restrictedness of his role and behavioural issues were a major problem and gave rise to the need for constant supervision:

> I can't leave her on her own because she forgets to do things, I can't trust her. (Mr Carson)

He felt that his mental health had suffered due to the demands of his role:

> It's the stress part of looking after her that affects you, you can't really settle down. (Mr Carson)

Although they had lived in the same rented house for 49 years, they had little contact with neighbours and didn't ask them for help. However, support was received from home carers who visited twice daily and from his daughter who lived locally.

Not only do older spouse carers form an increasingly significant proportion of unpaid carers and provide more intensive levels of care than younger counterparts but they are also likely to be caring for someone with dementia. Thus around half of carers aged 75 and over are dementia carers (Greenwood & Smith, 2016), often while dealing with health problems of their own (Morgan et al., 2020). As Vignette 4.1 highlights, this dementia care can carry with it particularly high demands and significant levels of restrictedness (Greenwood & Smith, 2016). In accordance with this, Johansson et al. (2022) found that behavioural stress, self-rated health and isolation were some of the most negative features of spousal caregiving for people with dementia. Due to the typically progressive nature of the dementia trajectory, the onset of these demands is likely to be an insidious process becoming more pronounced over the later life course (Turjamaa et al., 2020).

4.2   Perceptions

Attempts to measure the objective impact of or 'cost' of unpaid caring have reduced in popularity in recent years with the focus being shifted towards qualitative research methods and the subjective and nuanced meanings that carers attach to their role (Larkin et al., 2019). These meanings effect the way in which society, welfare agencies and carers themselves perceive and interpret their experiences and serve to 'structure' and 'mediate' the relationship between unpaid carers and service providers (Twigg & Atkin, 1994). These subjective perceptions will be further explored in this section.

4.2.1   Nuances

In their exploration of the diverse and subjective aspects of the unpaid caring experience, Twigg and Atkin (1994) distinguish between three individual responses. The first is the 'engulfment mode' in which the carer is highly involved and subordinates their life to that of the cared-for person. The second is the 'boundary setting mode' in which there remains an element of separation between the carer and their situation. Thirdly, is the 'symbiotic mode' in which carers gain in a positive way from their role to the extent that they would not wish their responsibilities to be taken away from them. In this respect, the objective and subjective demands of the caring role are not necessarily related, with the subjective impact of caring and caring strategies utilised being influenced not simply by the actual degree of caring responsibility but also by other more arbitrary factors. However, the general neglect of the experiences of older spouse carers means that the potentially unique features of their caring relationships have not been fully addressed.

With a view to redressing this neglect, Johansson et al. (2022) suggest that the spousal caring role is embedded within long term kinship and marital relationships which serve to mediate the experienced burden of this role. Allied with this is the commonly held perception of spousal caregiving as 'life sustaining' (Morgan et al., 2020) and as being part of the marriage contract in 'sickness and in health'. Enlarging the experiences of spouse carers, Johansson et al. (2022) identify positive aspects as including mutuality and emotional closeness, while negative aspects include behavioural stress, self-rated health and loneliness. They go on to suggest the need for responsive service interventions which help to sustain the caring relationship by accentuating its positive aspects while minimising negative components of this care. In their focus on the transition to dependency in older age, the gerontological concept of the 'fourth age' is also relevant to the way in which older spouse carers perceive their role. According to this perspective, attitudes of stoicism in the face of adversity are adopted by older people in order to maintain dignity and identity following the onset of infirmity (Lloyd et al., 2014). Although research on this issue has tended to focus on older people experiencing this onset themselves, a similar process is likely to be apparent amongst older spouse carers who are dealing with the transition to dependency of their partner while also potentially dealing with health problems of their own (Morgan et al., 2020).

In accordance with the above discussion, a nuanced view of caring and its incorporation of both positive and negative aspects was apparent in the accounts of many respondents and none maintained that they were wholly dissatisfied with their role. Moreover, while it was recognised that their life had changed, this was not often perceived to be a good thing or a bad thing, it was just different. Matters were further complicated by the fact that some carers felt that aspects of their life had simultaneously improved and worsened as a result of caring. For example, Mr Cicourel felt that while caring for his wife was mentally stressful, he would find not caring to be equally stressful due to the fact that he would be worried that she was receiving an adequate alternative source of care:

As long as she's OK, I'm OK. (Mr Cicourel)

Similarly, Mrs Reid felt that, in some respects her life had got worse as a result of the restrictedness of her caring role. However, in other respects it had got better as her membership of a carer support group had broadened her circle of friends. Her ambivalence is illustrated here:

> Some days I think that it's nice to have someone to talk to, then other days I think that I've spent my whole life caring for people. (MrsReid)

In addition, while most respondents appeared to adhere to 'symbiotic' models of care in which their life was willingly given over to their caring role (Twigg & Atkin, 1994), some carers apparently conformed to more than one model simultaneously. For example, Mr Wilson an 85-year-old spouse carer, while experiencing symbiosis in his role, also showed evidence of boundary setting, pursuing many leisure interests such as bowling and night classes. The fact that this pursuit was facilitated by the availability of domiciliary support serves to highlight the way in which the adoption of models of caring (Twigg & Atkin, 1994) are not only individually derived but are also mediated by access to resources. In spite of these many nuanced aspects of the caring role, some significant themes did emerge throughout the interviews on the positive and negative aspects of caring and these are outlined below.

4.2.2   Negatives

Regarding negative aspects of caring, a significant theme emerging was that of the various forms of restrictedness experienced by respondents, as highlighted in the previous section:

> Well we have always done everything together and it has got that we can't do the things that we want to. (Mrs Williams)

In addition, in accordance with gerontological themes of embodiment and the fourth age (Tulle, 2015), the performance of personal care was a further source of stress for carers. Such personal care has been identified by Twigg and Atkin (1994) as problematic. This is because its intimate nature can run counter to culturally prescribed expectations about acceptable physical contact even within the spousal relationship, potentially giving rise to distress and alienation. Thus Mr Cicourel recounted his embarrassment at having to provide intimate personal care such as washing and dressing to his wife:

> You see it was frustrating because washing a woman isn't like washing a man and then she was in the menopause as well. (Mr Cicourel)

Dealing with incontinence was also found to be one of the most stressful aspects of respondent's role:

> Putting him on the pot you know that's really the most unpleasant thing, to make sure he uses the lavatory before he goes out. I just stand there saying go on, go on. That is something I wish I could do without. (Mrs Field)

A further negative feature of some supervisory and personal care tasks was that they needed to be provided on demand rather than on a planned basis:

> I'm on hand 24 hours a day. I mean when we go to bed at night, sometimes she can manage to get out of bed so she can get on the commode, sometimes I'll have to get her out and then wait and put her back. Somebody's got to be with her, you couldn't leave her on her own. (Mr MacLellan)

This aspect of personal care put an additional pressure on carers who could also face the dilemma of determining the extent to which assistance should be given in the interests of maximising the independence of the care-recipient (Argyle, 2012). This could give rise to a tension between care and control and could also be perceived negatively by the cared for spouse who wanted to remain independent:

> Well the home carer, she'll wash her in the morning, sometimes, not always she'll manage to get her in the bath on her own and I'll leave the door open in case she needs me but she does manage to get in and out by herself. She doesn't get right in the bath, she's only got a seat to sit on about half way down and then I'll go and wash her back down and shower her and all that. She doesn't like that; she likes to be on her own if she can manage. (Mr MacLellan)

4.2.3   *Positives*

With regard to positive aspects of their role, the commonly occurring practical interdependence within the caring relationship could be interpreted as one such benefit. This practical interdependence has been found to be particularly common within the spousal care which is often seen as an extension of marital intimacy and companionship (Johansson et al., 2022). As a result of this interdependence, the distinction between the care giver and care receiver can become blurred and self- identification as a carer is less likely with the spousal rather than the caring relationship having primacy:

> You don't think of yourself as a carer until you sit down and think about what you're doing. (Mrs Reid)

Accompanying this practical interdependence is often an emotional interdependence. Consequently, while many respondents apparently subordinated their lives to that of the cared-for-person, they also experienced 'role symbiosis', due to the positive benefits experienced:

> I can't lead a life of my own, it's just all taken up with looking after Pete. I don't mind you see. We've been married nearly fifty years and we still love each other in sickness and in health. (Mrs Harris)

The incidence of reciprocity was also implicitly or explicitly referred to by spouse carers. Barnes (1997) identifies three types of reciprocity. Firstly the fulfilment of a sense of duty and the repayment of debt owed for past assistance. As Mr Tumin said of his wife:

> I just enjoy looking after her, I'm grateful, she had to look after me, she looked after me for six months when I had my hip done, now it's my turn. (Mr Tumin)

A second form of reciprocity can be seen to arise from the intrinsic psychological benefits gained from caring. For while feminists have tended to resist these positive interpretations of caring, many carers expressed such benefits including the sense of sustained purpose and a job well done, companionship and the opportunity to learn new skills:

It's not all bad. There's a certain satisfaction in looking after the patient and in knowing that you've done a good job. (Mrs Flude)

Such intrinsic satisfactions could derive from interpersonal and altruistic factors such as pleasure in the act of giving, the avoidance of guilt and the desire to feel wanted or needed. A third type of reciprocal exchange identified by Barnes (1997) is the belief held by carers that they are able to protect the cared for person from what they believe to be negative consequences or outcomes. As Mr Cicourel said of his twenty years' experience caring for his wife:

The doctor said it's surprising she's lasted so long. Well she's lasted so long because of the medication and because I've been looking after her. She wouldn't have lasted half as long as what she has done if she had been neglected. (Mr Cicourel)

These positive benefits and the interdependence within the caring relationship are highlighted by former spouse carers who commonly experience not a relief from burden but a great sense of loss not only of their partner but also of their identity and purpose in life. This is illustrated by the accounts of three male respondents who, when seen for their follow-up interviews, were no longer caring for their wives (Vignette 4.2).

Vignette 4.2: The Former Spouse Carers
Mr Cicourel who was 69, had been caring for his wife since she first developed multiple sclerosis 20 years ago with his role becoming progressively more intensive during this time as her physical condition worsened. Mr Caplow, an 87-year-old had also been caring for his wife for a long period, since she developed diverticulitis twelve years previously. Like Mrs Cicourel, her condition had progressively worsened and for the last six years of her life had left their flat only once. As well as performing highly demanding caring roles, both respondents had health problems of their own but largely attributed this to their advancing years:

(continued)

Vignette 4.2: (continued)

My health hasn't been affected and you don't get better as you get older, I'm full of aches and pains. (Mr Caplow)

I'm not as fit as I was ten years ago but that's the same with everyone. (Mr Cicourel)

Both also experienced restrictedness as a result of caring:

If you continue with your sports or whatever, you become frustrated because there is a time limit. (Mr Cicourel)

When Mr Caplow and Mr Cicourel were seen for follow-up interviews their wives had recently died and, contrary to oppressive concepts of caring, they both reported a significant sense of loss. An important aspect of this was in the loneliness and isolation which they felt, in spite of their attempts to pursue an active life outside the home:

I'm lonely, there's nothing that fills the space. I go out three or four times a week to the church hall to play snooker but when you come back the place is empty. (Mr Caplow)

I still play bowls and for a couple of hours, I forget everything and then I come back to an empty house. A house is a house, it's not a home. (Mr Cicourel)

Similar sentiments were expressed by Mr Hunter after his 90 year old wife who had dementia had been admitted to a care home in the previous year:

I'm in a state, I don't care if I go to sleep and don't wake up. (Mr Hunter)

The experiences of these former carers (Vignette 4.2) have been reflected in other research which suggests that such carers commonly experience ambivalence, a loss of purpose and loneliness following the termination of their caring role and that their continuing need for support is neither recognised or addressed (Watts & Cavaye, 2018). As Larkin and Milne (2017) observe, nor has the dynamic and changing nature of the post caring stage been fully recognised or the diverse ways in which this stage is experienced by different groups of carers. Thus for former spouse carers their perceived sense of loss is likely to be particularly significant, especially for those whose partner was admitted to a care home who may experience guilt as a result of this. This is due to the fact that their caring has taken place within a long term relationship and is likely to be mediated by the incidence of reciprocal exchanges and by social expectations of marital duty (Johansson et al., 2022).

The negative experiences of former carers combined with the positive aspects of the caring role potentially undermine portrayals of such caring as inevitably burdensome and adopted due to a lack of economic leverage with which to resist this role (Arber & Ginn, 1993). These experiences also highlight some of the unique features of this caring by older spouses and the high levels of interdependence commonly apparent within their caring relationships. The apparently high degree of commonality in this experience and the 'collective subjectivities' associated with this (Tanner, 2010) serve to undermine individualistic concepts of caring and the belief that the experience of this caring is idiosyncratic and self-defined. For as Parker (1993) observe, such experiences may be socially mediated and reflect social expectations of what carers should and should not do. The structured as well as individualistic elements of caring are further under lined by the fact that the caring 'models' (Twigg & Atkin, 1994) adopted by respondents were sometimes influenced by their access to resources such as the availability of substitute support helping carers to set boundaries in their role. It will be the purpose of the next chapter to further investigate the complex interaction between structure and constraint and action and meaning in the lives of respondents by exploring the influence of context and resources upon their experiences.

References

Argyle, E. (2012). Person centred dementia care: Problems and possibilities. *Working with Older People, 16*(2), 69–77.

Arber, S., & Ginn, J. (1993). Class, caring and the life-course. In S. Arber & M. Evandrou (Eds.), *Ageing, independence and the life-course* (pp. 149–168). Jessica Kingsley.

Barnes, M. (1997). *Care, communities and citizens.* Longman.

Carers UK. (2022). *State of caring 2022: A snapshot of unpaid care in the UK.* Carers UK.

Cooper, B., & Harrop, A. (2023). *Support guaranteed: The roadmap to a national care service.* Fabian Society.

Greenwood, N., & Smith, R. (2016). The oldest carers: A narrative review and synthesis of the experiences of carers aged over 75 years. *Maturitas, 94,* 161–172.

Johansson, M., McKee, K., Dahlberg, L., Summer Meranius, M., Williams, C., & Marmstål Hammar, L. (2022). Negative impact and positive value of caregiving in spouse carers of persons with dementia in Sweden. *International Journal of Environmental Research and Public Health, 19*(3), 1788.

Larkin, M., & Milne, A. (2017). What do we know about older former carers? Key issues and themes. *Health and Social Care in the Community, 25*(4), 396–1403.

Larkin, M., Henwood, M., & Milne, A. (2019). Carer related research and knowledge: Findings from a scoping review. *Health and Social Care in the Community, 27*(1), 55–67.

Lloyd, L., Calnan, M., Cameron, A., Seymour, J., & Smith, R. (2014). Identity in the fourth age: Perseverance, adaptation and maintaining dignity. *Ageing and Society, 34*(1), 1–19.

Morgan, T., Bharmal, A., Duschinsky, R., & Barclay, S. (2020). Experiences of oldest-old caregivers whose partner is approaching end-of-life: A mixed-method systematic review and narrative synthesis. *PLoS One, 15*(6), e0232401.

Office for National Statistics. (2022, June 28). Census 2021 Statistics, First results from Census 2021 in England and Wales.

Parker, G. (1993). *With this body: Caring and disability in marriage.* Open University Press.

Purkis, M., & Ceci, C. (2015). Problematizing care burden research. *Ageing and Society, 35*(7), 1410–1428.

Tanner, D. (2010). *Managing the ageing experience: Learning from older people.* Policy Press.

Tulle, E. (2015). Theorising embodiment and ageing. In J. Twigg & W. Martin (Eds.), *Routledge handbook of cultural gerontology* (pp. 125–132). Routledge.

Turjamaa, R., Salpakari, J., & Koskinen, L. (2020). Experiences of older spousal caregivers for caring a person with a memory disorder. *Healthcare, 8*(2), 95.

Twigg, J., & Atkin, K. (1994). *Carers perceived.* Open University Press.

Twigg, J., & Martin, W. (Eds.). (2015). *Routledge handbook of cultural gerontology.* Routledge.

Watts, J., & Cavaye, J. (2018). Being a former carer: Impacts on health and well-being. *Illness, Crisis and Loss, 26*(4), 330–345.

CHAPTER 5

Context, Resources and Older Spouse Carers

Abstract Due to the fragmentation of research into unpaid caring and older age and its commonly adopted individualised focus, the interaction between structure and constraint on one hand and meaning and action on the other has been neglected especially with regard to the experiences of older spouse carers. It will be the purpose of this chapter to explore these issues by focusing on the way in which access to resources and contextual factors more generally can influence the experience of caring.

Keywords Money • Finances • Resources • Environment • Socio-economic status • Caregivers

Previous chapters have shown that there is a strong link between poverty and caring with many carers experiencing high levels of material deprivation due to the financial costs incurred as a result of their role (Carers UK, 2022). However, like the link between the objective and subjective experience of caring, the relationship between poverty and caring is a complex one. For not only can caring cause material deprivation but this deprivation can also influence the experience of caring with financial constraints and unfavourable environments potentially serving to exacerbate the demands experienced by unpaid carers (Morgan, 2018). These neglected issues will be explored throughout the rest of this chapter.

5.1   Household Assets

In accordance with second generation approaches to older age and more recently developed concepts of 'precarity' (Grenier et al., 2021) and 'social risk' (Morgan, 2018), the context of caring and access to household resources can go on to affect the role of older carers. In spite of this, research into unpaid care has not only been characterised by an ageless analysis but also by a classless analysis and a subsequent neglect of the influence of socio-economic factors on the caring role (Arber & Ginn, 1993).

5.1.1   Financial Issues

The neglect of context and resources in research into unpaid caring has been compounded by the individualised and fragmented nature of this research. For in its focus on the diverse and subjective meanings of carers, it has overlooked the influence of material constraint on their lives and the potential social risk arising from it (Morgan, 2018). As Grenier et al. (2021) recognise, a similar neglect has been apparent in gerontological research. For the recent focus on diversity in later life neglects the way in which the experience of frailty and dependence in this stage of life is socially structured by such things as poverty and the subsequent 'precarity' that can be experienced. Consequently, while there appears to be an increasing polarity in the financial position of older people due to such things as the growth of occupational pensions amongst the better off, many older people continue to live on very limited post-retirement incomes. Thus most respondents in this research experienced a drop in income following retirement. In spite of this they were sometimes reluctant to apply for benefits to which they were entitled with £2.2 billion of such benefits going unclaimed each year (Age UK, 2022). For example, Mr MacLellan recounted his decision not to apply for relevant benefits:

> I didn't bother because we manage anyway, we don't spend anything. (Mr MacLellan)

Other carers spoke at length of the way in which they had reduced their spending in order to adjust to their limited income:

> You reduce yourself to it. If you live in the fast lane and then you come in the slow lane. If you adjust the speed then you're OK...You just have to cut out the trimmings, there's a hell of a lot that you don't really need. (Mr Cicourel)

An implication of their tendency to cut back on their spending was that it increased the restrictedness which carers experienced:

> We don't go anywhere or do anything, it (household income) just goes on food and the upkeep of this house. (Mr Hunter)

> That costs money to go out and drink and smoke and we don't go out so that's why we can live comfortably. (Mr Phillips)

> We manage as far as money's concerned because we don't go anywhere or do anything so you can't spend anything can you. (Mr MacLellan)

As previous research has recognised, these financial constraints can not only influence the restrictedness that carers experience, it can also influence the incidence of caring with high intensity caring being much more common amongst poorer groups around the world. The influence of resources on unpaid caring is clearly illustrated by UK based official statistics which show a close relationship between the incidence of social deprivation and of high intensity unpaid caring (Office for National Statistics, 2023). Similar trends have been found internationally with the OECD (Colombo et al., 2011) observing that poverty rates amongst intensive caregivers around the world is twice as high than for non- intensive carers. This close correlation between high levels of unpaid caring and relative deprivation can be seen as partly attributable to the similar correlation between this deprivation and the incidence of ill health and disability, which in turn increases the need for unpaid care. As Arber and Ginn (1993) suggest, it can also be attributable to financial interdependence and the reduced ability experienced by the less well-off to resist the demands of unpaid caring. For carers in this research, this financial interdependence was substantiated by follow-up interviews when, for some carers their position had changed, the cared-for person either having died or admitted into permanent care. All of the carers in this situation reported a significant decline in their household income, as two bereaved carers stated:

> My income went down by half you see, there's lighting and gas, the telephone still to pay out of that little bit. It's easier to live as a couple than a single person on their own. It's cheaper. (Mr Caplow)

> My income has dropped now to less than half of what we were getting. (Mr Cicourel)

This financial interdependence could not only increase the need to pool limited household resources, it could also undermine the choice and spontaneity which has been identified as crucial in maintaining the intrinsic value of the informal caring role (Parker, 1981). The role of financial concerns in promoting the incidence of high intensity caring is well illustrated by the case of Mrs Flude who was dissatisfied with her caring role which she felt was had been imposed on her solely as a result of financial constraint (Vignette 5.1).

Vignette 5.1: The Financially Dependent Spouse Carer
Mrs Flude was 68 and cared for her husband who had dementia. She felt that financial concerns played an important role in shaping her caring responsibilities, describing how she had downsized from her previous house in order to pay off her husband's gambling debts:

> So apart from the emotional stress and shock of him being so ill, I couldn't see how I was going to manage financially. Because I had already moved from a bigger house because we hadn't enough money. So I already had to move with great stress to a lesser house if you like to get some capital to pay off debts. (Mrs Flude)

Due to ongoing money worries she was also deterred from having her husband admitted into residential care due to the fact that she would have lost the income she needed to remain in their current marital home:

> If he had gone into care I would have lost my home. They would have taken his occupational pension, his Attendance Allowance and his old age pension, so that would have left me with nothing except my old age pension, which is very little. (Mrs Flude)

Mrs Flude claimed to have had long term poor relationships with her husband and was highly dissatisfied with her role:

> It's no life except that I now get respite care. I have a lot of financial worries. (Mrs Flude)

The experiences of Mrs Flude (Vignette 5.1) highlight the way in which unpaid care is not necessarily an expressive, spontaneous and positive experience but may be instrumental, coerced and oppressive as a result of financial concerns (Arber & Ginn, 1993). Moreover, in spite of postmodern assertions of increasing affluence in older age (Gilleard & Higgs, 2000), these concerns continue to persist in older age. Thus Age UK (2022) has found that 18 percent of pensioners in the UK currently live in poverty and this represents a rise since 2013–2014 when those in poverty formed 14 percent of the pensioner population.

5.1.2   *Material Resources*

Resource based issues can not only constrain choice in the assumption of a caring role, they can also influence the way in which this care is provided and the demands experienced as a result of this (Argyle, 2001). This is due the lack of access to material goods and services helping to alleviate these demands. Statistics show that this lack of access is likely to disproportionately affect older people with Age UK finding that the common incidence of relative poverty in older age is also reflected in access to these material goods and services. Thus 7 percent of older in the UK are unable to afford access to a car or taxi when needed and with older people being generally less likely than younger counterparts to have access to household goods and technology (Age UK, 2022). In accordance with the fact that it is not only income but also access to other material resources which can influence the experience of caring (Arber & Ginn, 1993), access to private transport emerged as a resource highly valued by respondents helping to ease the demands of their caring role and to maintain and extend their social life and networks:

> Well if I didn't have a car, I wouldn't get her out. I mean I use it to go to the shop because I suffer from angina. (Mr MacLellan)

However, out of all the carers in the sample, only six had a car and even those who did often struggled to maintain them on their limited post-retirement incomes:

> We've got a car stuck in the garage. It's never been out since he had this stroke. It needs repairing but I can't afford to get the mechanic in, I don't know how much it's going to cost. (Mrs Gibbons)

Social trends such as the growth of out of town developments and the fall in public transport provision have led to an increasing reliance on this car ownership (Rowles & Bernard, 2013). This development is likely to disadvantage older people, who are less likely than younger counterparts to be car owners and who often experience other mobility impairments:

> You see we can't get out and we don't have a car, we never have, and we can't walk far. (Mrs Lane)

Due to these mobility restrictions, respondents without access to private transport were often forced to rely on more expensive alternatives:

> Neither of us can walk very far, if we want to go to hospital or to the doctors, we have to have a taxi. (Mrs Taylor)

In addition to access to transport, adequate housing is another resource that is likely to have an important impact on the experience of unpaid caring and is likely to give rise to socio-economic differences in this experience. For example, Mr MacLellan who lived in a one bedroomed rented flat found it difficult to manoeuvre his wife's wheelchair within the confined space. Sleeping was also difficult because of his wife's restlessness:

> We had a double bed when we first came here but I couldn't sleep with her because of her shaking. It makes it a bit tighter with two single beds. I could do with a bit more room. (Mr MacLellan)

Moreover, as the only social housing tenant in the sample with his own car, due to lack of nearby parking facilities, until recently, Mr MacLellan had been forced to walk over a hundred yards from his flat to reach his car when he wanted to use it. This exertion, he said, exacerbated his angina:

> I've got a garage now, which is only just across the road. I'm coping pretty well now. When I had a distance to walk it got a bit dodgy. (Mr MacLellan)

Socio-economic differences are not only apparent in the housing environment. They are also thought to be apparent in the attitudes adopted towards housing with some theorists believing that tenants are much less emotionally attached to their homes than their owner-occupying counterparts (Rowles & Bernard, 2013). Indeed many owner-occupiers expressed such an attachment with Mrs Field explaining how she refused to move house even though she recognised that her current house was now too big for her needs:

> I've got used to the space. A friend who died aged 94, he lived on his own, he said, 'you know quite well you'll never leave there until one of you is carried out feet first' and I said, 'yes I expect you're right', unless my husband gets so bad that he has to go into respite permanently, in which case I would have to sell the house as it's too big. (Mrs Field)

However, not only does this theory fail to take account of international variations in attitudes towards housing status, it also implies that, due to their allegedly low attachment to their homes, tenants can be relocated to other housing with minimum personal distress and disruption (Rowles & Bernard, 2013). However, contrary to this assumption, both renters and home owners tended to perceive relocation in a negative light. This could be due to pragmatic factors such as leaving behind familiar and well-established neighbourhood networks. It could also be due to the fact that relocation in older age is more likely to be perceived as a negative transition, rather than a positive progression and is often brought on by the onset of disability (Rowles & Bernard, 2013). In accordance with this, Mrs Taylor, a social housing tenant spoke of how she missed the garden of her former rented home:

> We had a very long garden. We had to leave there because we couldn't get upstairs because of the angina, that's why we came here. I miss it very much because when it was nice we used to go out and sit on the lawn. I never get any fresh air. (Mrs Taylor)

While both owner occupiers and renters appeared to share negative perceptions of rehousing, respondents who were renters were more likely to have to undergo this experience due to their lesser ability to acquire aids and adaptations which would help them to remain in their existing home (Rowles & Bernard, 2013). Social housing tenants also experienced a lesser degree of control over the rehousing process thus serving to exacerbate their levels of distress and reducing their choice in the type and location of housing allocated to them. For unlike owner-occupiers, they were largely reliant on housing bureaucracy to organise this rehousing and often found themselves "waiting for someone to die", as one respondent put it.

5.2   THE WIDER ENVIRONMENT

The previous section has focused on the household resources available to carers and their influence on the experience of caring. Also important is the wider context within which caring takes place including the availability of external support and the social, economic and policy trends that may influence this (Cooper & Harrop, 2023). It will thus be seen in this section how economic and social factors as well as developments in social welfare provision have influenced the nature of this support.

5.2.1   *Consumerisation and Instrumentalisation*

Recent years have seen the growth of neo-liberal trends in welfare which have been characterised by the growth of a system of welfare pluralism, a marginalisation of the role of the state in service provision and the increasing targeting and consumerisation of this provision (Cooper & Harrop, 2023). Coupled with this has been the growth of personalised approaches to assessment and intervention with the goal of maximising the independence of those in receipt of these interventions. While the stated aims of these developments have been to promote service choice, flexibility and person centred approaches, as it has been seen in preceding chapters, they can run counter to the needs and aspirations of older people. For due to attitudes of stoicism (Lloyd et al., 2014), they may be reluctant to assume the role of active consumers 'shopping around' for services meaning that services are only accessed when a crisis point is reached. While for older spouse carers this reluctance may be compounded by the commonly occurring interdependence within their caring relationships. The limited incomes and financial caution of older spouse carers may form a further barrier to access due to an inability or unwillingness to pay the charges that are increasingly being incurred for such services. Thus Cooper and Harrop (2023) have found that older people in the most deprived areas are twice as likely to lack the support that they need those in the least deprived areas. For example, a 69-year-old carer, Mr Cicourel, described how he was unable to afford a home sitting service for his wife as his relatively low income meant that he did not feel able to afford the hourly fee which he was being asked to pay:

They said, 'Have you got any money'. I said 'Yes I've got a little bit put by' and they said 'In that case you'll have to pay towards it' and I said, 'Oh, I'm not bothered'. (Mr Cicourel)

This contrasted with the position of better-off carers who were able to purchase outside help. For example, Mr Hunter described how he for many years he had employed domestic help:

I just wash up and do a bit of cleaning now and again when it's necessary because we pay for two cleaners to come in. (Mr Hunter)

However, even better off carers were sometimes reluctant to pay for outside help. For example, although Mrs Field could afford to pay for such help to assist in the care of her husband, she had to be persuaded by her daughter to employ a temporary live in carer from an agency to give her a rest from caring when she was ill:

They send out people to take over the whole house but they are extremely expensive. Anyway my daughter said that we shall have to regard this as a holiday, don't do anything just let the staff get on with it. (Mrs Field)

Consequently, the willingness to pay for outside help may not simply be the product of material circumstances but also due to cultural and attitudinal factors such as financial caution and the degree of familiarity with the type of help employed (Argyle & Warren, 2005). Access to information and cultural capital more generally could have a further impact on the ability of carers to access help. As such, confusion about the accessibility or availability of services was expressed by a number of carers, thus as Mrs Taylor stated with regard to accessing a free bus service:

We see all these buses going past but we can't seem to get the knack of them. Nobody's really been plain enough to tell us what you've got to do to get these buses. (Mrs Taylor)

Financial issues not only influenced access to formal support, it also potentially influenced access to informal help from kin and non-kin. This could be due to the relative lack of choice that tenants experienced in process of rehousing. It could also be due to such things as the increasing instrumentalisation of informal help through the need to provide material reward for this help. This issue of instrumentalisation can be seen as an embodiment of the increasingly individualistic and narcissistic nature of such relationships as alluded to by third generation theorists (Gilleard & Higgs, 2000). It also undermines the perception informal support as being based on expressive feelings rather than instrumental reward as some theorists have maintained (Parker, 1981).

In accordance with this move towards the instrumentalisation of informal support, interviews revealed the high incidence of material reward being given by carers to informal supporters in return for their practical help. For example, the daughter of spouse carer, Mr Carson, gave up her job so that she could assist in the care of her mother and for her 'wages' she was given her mother's Attendance Allowance:

> You see my daughter used to work and when the Attendance Allowance came through I said why not give up your job and work for me. It's just the same as paying someone else to come in isn't it. She comes in practically every day. She definitely looks after me. (Mr Carson)

Another spouse carer, Mrs Coates, gave her son who lived in London her entire state pension every week in return for the occasional help which he provided with shopping and gardening:

> I give my pension to Charles for his help. He pays the gardener. (Mrs Coates)

Finances were not the only form of payment used with Mr and Mrs Lane signing over the house to their son in return for the help that he provided:

> Actually the house isn't ours, we gave it to our son ten years ago, he's such a lot of help, he does all the repairs. It took the responsibility off us. (Mrs Lane)

In addition, Mrs Field let her gardener's wife have free use of her car in return for regular 'chauffeuring duties':

> I said I think I've got a good idea. I said, you take my car and keep it in your garage and take responsibility for it, use it when you want. In return, perhaps you could take me about to the hospital and things like that. (Mrs Field)

Research has found that such instrumental exchanges can help to promote acceptable boundaries and feelings of self-esteem and independence amongst older people. Conversely, self-perceptions of dependency appear to be related to feelings of having nothing of value to exchange, with the result that those most needing care may be least likely to be able to reciprocate (Langan et al., 1996). As such contrary to mutually supportive portrayals of working class life (Young & Willmott, 1962), poverty and the social marginalisation arising from it can actually undermine informal caring networks by reducing the incentive and ability of poor people to maintain such networks. For example, Mr Cicourel complained that he only saw his wife's relatives when they wanted some sort of help, which he was unwilling or unable to provide:

> The only time I see them is if they want a favour or if they want anything.
> (Mr Cicourel)

5.2.2   Neighbourhood and Networks

Just as relative poverty can undermine access to formal and informal support, it can also effect the neighbourhood and networks of older spouse carers with implications for their caring role. Thus as it has been seen in previous chapters, contrary to postmodern claims of increasing social diversity, there tends to be a high concentration of high intensity carers in areas with high levels of social deprivation while low intensity caring tends to be more geographically dispersed (Office for National Statistics, 2023). This can partly be attributed to the close correlation between social deprivation on one hand and disability and ill health on the other. It can also be due to the lesser ability of poorer people to 'resist' a highly demanding caring role (Arber & Ginn, 1993). Due to a similar lack of choice and control in the process of rehousing, tenants are more likely than owner occupiers to find themselves in areas far removed from established networks (Rowles & Bernard, 2013). A further notable aspect of the environmental disadvantage experienced by some tenants which emerged from interviews was the fear of or incidence of crime as well as violence and harassment from neighbours. No owner-occupiers reported such problems as compared to several tenants, some of whom spoke of severe harassment and antisocial behaviour which was reported to the police:

I've had some bad neighbours. They've been in five years and they've just evicted them. There were four children from 9 to 15 and they were jumping through windows and throwing stuff – a rolling pin came through a few weeks ago. Just before they went, these kids they had guns and they were up trees shooting windows out. (Mr Hall)

There was a stage when we couldn't even sit here and look out the window. We had eggs thrown at the window, we had paint thrown at the window stones thrown at the window. I fetched the police; I kept ringing for the police. (Mrs Phillips)

Another social housing tenant spoke of the general unfriendliness of his neighbours:

I mean you don't know people, you think you do but you don't. I mean I was walking down there and there were two ladies I knew who walked past me and they never even spoke. They knew where I was going because I was going to the same place. You notice things like that. (Mr Caplow)

Linked with the issue of neighbourhood is that of social isolation which was experienced by many respondents:

We don't go on holiday, we don't go out drinking. (Mrs Phillips)

I don't go out a lot spending money, well I don't really go out. (Mrs Lipset)

This issue of social isolation in older age has long been a subject of debate within social gerontology. For first generation approaches this isolation is seen as an inevitable result of the process of ageing which results in a 'social disengagement' from former roles due to the onset of infirmity and implicitly regards this process as transcending socio-economic status (Cumming & Henry, 1962). In contrast, second generation approaches regards this isolation as socially structured as a result of such things as limited post-retirement incomes (Phillipson, 1982, 2013). In accordance with this latter view, the social isolation of respondents appeared to be at least partially financially derived. Thus such things as the lack of money to pay for relief care, the lack of access to a car and a general unwillingness to spend their money on anything but the necessities of life prevented respondents from maintaining or extending their social networks. For example, Mr Tumin, an 84-year-old carer described how in his sixties not only did he retire and sever all contact with former work colleagues but he also left the ex-service men's association, of which he had been an active member and sold his car leading to a massive reduction in his social life:

> We never socialised as such since I retired. I had a car up to then, well after a couple of years, it was stuck on the door and I was paying all that money and then going on the bus, so I flogged it. (Mr Tumin)

His motives behind these actions appeared to be financially based in that he didn't feel able to afford to be as socially active as he was when he was working. However, for some respondents it was unclear whether lack of a car was a symptom or a cause of social isolation with some car owners explaining how they sold their cars following retirement as they felt they didn't need them as they never went out anyway:

> We don't go out like we used to, we used to go out in the car, we used petrol and that sort of thing but we don't go out at all now. (Mrs Coates)

Similarly, Mrs Field, who was a car owner, attributed her propensity not to go out to a general characteristic of older people:

> I'm very idle and stay at home all the time and only go out occasionally. We don't want to go out, we get lazy and stop in. Have you noticed that with other older people? Can't make the effort. (Mrs Field)

Consequently, unlike the experiences of many younger people in poverty, the isolation of older carers was potentially compounded by their own age and disability as well as that of their spouse with such issues being regularly referred to when respondents spoke of mobility issues:

> We could afford to run (the car) but Pete got this thing and I got this osteoporosis – we just couldn't cope so we got rid of it. (Mrs Harris)

> It's just that we can't get about, if we lived at the top near buses it would be better but it's ages since we went on a bus, it's just that walking from here to the bus stop, so I never bother, I don't go out. (Mrs Taylor)

The way in which car ownership and mobility issues are potentially mediated not only by access to material resources and the restrictedness arising from caring but also by physical pathology is well illustrated by the case of Mr Hunter (Vignette 5.2).

Vignette 5.2: The 89-Year-Old Car Driver

Mr Hunter was an 89 year old middle class carer who had been driving for 72 years, often in the course of his former occupation as a master butcher. When seen for his initial interview, Mr Hunter had a car but rarely used it, relying instead on his son for most of his transportation needs. The reasons for this were not financial but due to his age, for while he felt himself to be in generally good health, he nevertheless, did not feel competent to drive:

> I have a car but I don't use it and I'm getting rid of it because well I don't think I could get another licence at my age. At my age your reactions are not quick enough really. (Mr Hunter)

Indeed, when seen for his follow-up interview he had sold his car and replaced it with a mobility scooter. Although, as one of the better off respondents, Mr Hunter was fortunate in that he could afford a mobility scooter, as it can be seen, it was age related physical impairment rather than financial issues that influenced his decision to sell his car.

As the experiences of Mr Hunter illustrate (Vignette 5.2), the isolation of respondents potentially transcended socio-economic factors and could also be due to age related issues such as disability. This is supported by research from around the world which shows that social isolation is common amongst all older spouse carers regardless of their socio-economic status (Ornstein et al., 2019). Similarly, Age UK (2022) has found that while 18 percent of older people did not go out socially at least once a month and 36 percent did not go on holiday, the most commonly given reason for this was health or disability rather than lack of money. These multiple issues potentially influencing the lives of older spouse carers serve to override the theoretical divides that have characterised research into older age and unpaid caring, suggesting the need for a theoretically integrated approach. This ongoing theme will be further explored in the next chapter which focuses on the way in which older spouse carers actively manage their caring role.

REFERENCES

Age UK. (2022). *Poverty in later life*. Age UK.

Arber, S., & Ginn, J. (1993). Class, caring and the life-course. In S. Arber & M. Evandrou (Eds.), *Ageing, independence and the life-course* (pp. 149–168). Jessica Kingsley.

Argyle, E. (2001). Poverty, disability and the role of older carers. *Disability and Society, 16*(4), 585–595.

Argyle, E., & Warren, L. (2005). *Older people and their money: Issues for policy and participation*. Cash and Care Conference, University of York. Retrieved May 24, 2023, from https://doi.org/10.13140/RG.2.2.13295.23209

Carers UK. (2022). *State of caring 2022: A snapshot of unpaid care in the UK*. Carers UK.

Colombo, F., Llena-Nozal, A., Mercier, J., & Tjadens, F. (2011). *Help wanted? Providing and paying for long-term care*. OECD Health Policy Studies, OECD Publishing.

Cooper, B., & Harrop, A. (2023). *Support guaranteed: The roadmap to a national care service*. Fabian Society.

Cumming, E., & Henry, W. (1962). *Growing old: The process of disengagement*. Basic Books.

Gilleard, C., & Higgs, P. (2000). *Cultures of ageing: Self, citizen and the body*. Prentice Hall.

Grenier, A., Phillipson, C., & Settersten, A. (Eds.). (2021). *Precarity and ageing: Understanding insecurity and risk in later life*. Bristol.

Langan, J., Means, R., & Rolfe, S. (1996). *Maintaining independence in later life: Older people speaking*. Anchor Trust.

Lloyd, L., Calnan, M., Cameron, A., Seymour, J., & Smith, R. (2014). Identity in the fourth age: Perseverance, adaptation and maintaining dignity. *Ageing and Society, 34*(1), 1–19.

Morgan, F. (2018). The treatment of informal care-related risks as social risks: An analysis of the English care policy system. *Journal of Social Policy, 47*(1), 179–196.

Office for National Statistics. (2023, February 13). Census 2021 Statistics, *Unpaid care by age sex and deprivation in England and Wales*.

Ornstein, K., Wolff, J., Bollens-Lund, E., Rahman, O., & Kelley, A. (2019). Spousal caregivers are caregiving alone in the last years of life. *Health Affairs, 38*(6), 964–972.

Parker, R. (1981). *Tending and social policy*. Policy Studies Institute.

Phillipson, C. (1982). *Capitalism and the construction of old age*. Macmillan.

Phillipson, C. (2013). *Ageing*. John Wiley and Sons.

Rowles, G., & Bernard, M. (Eds.). (2013). *Environmental gerontology: Making meaningful places in old age*. Springer Publishing Company.

Young, M., & Willmott, P. (1962). *Family and kinship in East London*. Penguin.

CHAPTER 6

The Management Strategies of Older Spouse Carers

Abstract Having explored the experience of caring and the influence of context and resources on this experience, in preceding chapters, this chapter will examine the way in which the caring role is actively managed by older spouse carers. As such, it will be shown how the lives of respondents were significantly transformed as a result of their caring role and the subsequent management strategies adopted. The first part of the chapter will focus on the adaptations and transitions experienced by older spouse carers and this will be followed by an exploration of the culture of coping that they commonly exhibit.

Keywords Coping • Stoicism • Caution • Transformations • Adaptation • Attitude

Contrary to the assumptions of early generations of gerontological thought which have tended to portray older people as being the passive victims of adverse circumstances (Cumming & Henry, 1962), older spouse carers do not simply passively react to these circumstances but actively adapt to them. As it has been shown in previous chapters, these modes of adaptation can be influenced by such things as physical pathology, material constraint and cultural and attitudinal issues rendering their experiences unique as compared to other groups of carers (Morgan et al., 2020). This chapter will further explore these modes of adaptation and management strategies utilised.

6.1   ADAPTATIONS AND TRANSFORMATIONS

With regard to the modes of adaptation employed by older spouse carers, in their review of relevant literature, Morgan et al. (2020) have identified some major themes. These include the theme of 'learning to care' due to the need to assume new and unfamiliar roles within the spousal relationship. Issues relating to their 'conceptualisation of their role' are also identified. These tend to be characterised by a struggle for continuity in the context of change and the maintenance of a process of 'biographical flow' in which familiar routines are maintained in order to minimise the impact of ill health and disability on their lives.

6.1.1   Continuity and Change

In accordance with the findings of previous research (Morgan et al., 2020), all respondents in this research experienced significant role transitions as a result of their caring responsibilities and some admitted to struggling to adapt to these changes:

> You do get so fed up with it, it gets on your nerves, it does get on your nerves. You can't do a damn thing about it. (Mr MacLellan)

> These past few years I do everything, its hard work housework you know. (Mr Hall)

For older spouse carers, this struggle to adapt and the role transitions accompanying this tends to be an insidious process which becomes more pronounced during the post-retirement phase thus running counter to perception of this stage of life as being unitary and unchanging (Twigg & Martin, 2015). For example, the illness of Mr Cicourel's wife who had multiple sclerosis had commenced while he was still working and the progressive deterioration of her condition meant that the onset of his caring role had been gradual:

I do what I can. I don't let her do cooking and things like that. I'm afraid she has burnt herself on occasions. When I was working it was difficult. Mind you, you can forget about that now. (Mr Cicourel)

Moreover, as these role transitions tended to be accelerated by the increasing disability of the cared-for person, they tended to be the most pronounced amongst the oldest carers in the sample. The fact that such older carers were also likely to experience the 'dual jeopardy' of having health problems of their own made their efforts at adaptation all the more notable (Morgan et al., 2020). As the following 91-year-old male spouse carer described his changing household responsibilities:

She used to do the shopping and things like that, cooking and looking after the house, I was just the provider, the gardener and the helper but she developed this arthritis of the spine which meant that shopping was getting very, very difficult, so I just took over. (Mr Tunstall)

In their maintenance of 'biographical flow', older spouse carers have been found to place a great emphasis on the home and the household when discussing the care they provide. This is because it helps to provide a familiar point of reference and counters the huge transformations apparent in other areas of their life (Morgan et al., 2020).

The routine of the house is exactly the same as when she ran it and it's just the same. I clean it the same. I shampoo the carpets and things like that. Brought up in service she was very strict about the home and she got me into it being strict like that and I do everything for the home the same as she did. (Mr Tumin)

I still put her housekeeping money out each week but instead of her paying for stuff, I take the money out instead. (Mr Tunstall)

This pursuance of stability in adverse circumstances and the significance of household routines in this process are highlighted by the practical interdependence commonly found within the caring relationships of older spouses. Indeed for the two couples identified below it was impossible to distinguish between the carer and cared for person within their respective relationships (Vignette 6.1).

Vignette 6.1: The Practically Interdependent Spouse Carers
Mr and Mrs Taylor were aged 92 and 84 respectively and regarded themselves as being involved in a two-way caring relationship. They both had heart problems as well as sight and mobility impairments. In accordance with their reciprocal roles, they shared household tasks with Mrs Taylor doing the cooking while Mr Taylor went to the shops and collected their pensions:

I pay the bills. (Mr Taylor)

And I do the housekeeping. (Mrs Taylor)

I don't want her thinking and worrying about bills coming in. I worry about them. (Mr Taylor)

He worries about that and I take out what I need. (Mrs Taylor)

Mr and Mrs Lane both of whom were 86 and who also had mobility impairments performed similarly complimentary household roles:

He washes the pots; I do a bit of cooking. We both help one another and if we aren't well, we just sit down and let it go. (Mrs Lane)

The Taylors' complimentary roles could be seen as relatively long standing. In contrast, for the Lanes, this role interdependency started only two years previously after Mr Lane had a heart attack. Prior to that he had been the main carer for his wife who had been ill for over ten years following a knee injury:

I used to have a housekeeping allowance. In fact I sometimes joke that I've never got any money and he says, well you know where it is if you want it. Yes but since I went into hospital, he took over and I never took it back. (Mrs Lane)

This practical interdependence commonly found in the caring relationship of older spouses as illustrated by Vignette 6.1 helps to highlight the many transformations often apparent in the lives of older spouse carers (Andréasson et al., 2023; Morgan et al., 2020). This interdependence also runs counter to the false dichotomy often placed between the needs of carers and care receivers (Barnes, 1997) and tends to be especially apparent when ill health is experienced by the older spouse carer themselves (Morgan et al., 2020).

6.1.2 Role Transitions

Associated with the high levels of adaptation apparent in the lives of older spouse carers is the need to learn new skills due to the performance of unfamiliar tasks (Morgan et al., 2020). More specific aspects of this learning have been identified by Carers UK (2022) with skills acquired by carers of all ages including empathy, resilience, advocacy, risk and time and financial management, communication skills and partnership working. For older spouse carers in particular, learning could also extend to protecting their partners dignity and autonomy both in terms of the performance of practical tasks (Andréasson et al., 2023) as well as in the decision making process and the support that is provided as part of this process (Fetherstonhaugh et al., 2019). For most spouses in this research, a carer dominated decision making style was adopted and for some this dominance represented a continuation of the style adopted earlier in their marriage. For example, Mrs Coates maintained that throughout their marriage she had always assumed control of her husband's income due to the fact that he was Polish and therefore unfamiliar with local currency:

> He's never had any money sense. He's from Poland, he's never understood English money. (Mrs Coates)

However transitions in decision making control usually involved a transformation of the roles and strategies previously adopted:

> She can't distinguish a five pence piece from a ten pence piece or copper from silver because she can't see it. Actually she's no money sense at all now, I look after all hers. If there's any problem now, it's actually deciding what we want. I have to do the thinking for her as well as the actual buying. (Mr Tunstall)

In spite of the widespread tendency for spouse carers to dominate the decision making process, such carers also use a variety of support strategies including consultation, discussion and the use of verbal and non-verbal cues to facilitate some level of mutual involvement in this process

(Fetherstonhaugh et al., 2019). This involvement is particularly apparent when decisions over minor issues are involved such as dietary choices rather than more major and complex decisions such as those involving finances where the carer is more likely to take sole control (Argyle & Warren, 2005). However, the nature of the decision making support provided can be a source of conflict with carers often having to negotiate the fine line between facilitation on one hand and imposition on the other (Fetherstonhaugh et al., 2019). Thus, they may provide too little support and overestimate the decision making capacity of their partner. Alternatively, too much or inappropriate support may be provided as a result of the carers underestimation of their partners capabilities or due to a wish to gain control within the caring relationship.

These transitions in decision making processes along with other practical responsibilities held by older spouse carers tend to be accompanied by a blurring of the traditional gender role divisions that characterised carers' earlier married lives (Morgan et al., 2020). This is clearly apparent in the reversal of the gendered nature of caring in older age with the traditional predominance of female carers being progressively equalised over the later life course. For while younger women are far more likely to be carers than younger men this gender divide is reversed in older age with men over 80 being slightly more likely to be carers than women of the same age group (Office for National Statistics, 2023). Blurring is also apparent in the roles performed with spousal carers having to take on their partner's former domains such as housework, shopping and money management. As two older male carers said of their wives:

> She's not done any shopping for twenty years. When she was OK she did. I mean we had a family, that's why she never worked as she was looking after a family. I mean I do it all now, cooking, cleaning, the lot. (Mr MacLellan)

> I never had anything to do with house finance, I gave her the money and she ruled the house with it but I've had to learn, when you're thrown in at the deep end, you've got to swim. (Mr Tumin)

As such the roles assumed often starkly contrasted with the traditional gender role expectations within marriage that characterised respondents formative years and which derived from the twin ideals of a wage earning husband and a caring and home based wife (Finch & Groves, 1983):

When we got married that was the way it was, nobody expected your wife to go out to work in those days, you got married and you had a family and usually the woman had plenty of work in the house. In those days there weren't the things that they have today, washing machines and all that kind of thing, the washing would take them two days and then there's children. I think if a woman's got children I think she's got plenty to do to look after them. (Mr MacLellan)

She ran the house, completely ran the house. I didn't do a thing about it. We were old fashioned. She was the housewife and she did the job. She wouldn't have it any other way. (Mr Tumin)

In spite of this gender equalisation of caring in older age and the increasing entry of women into the workplace, some feminists argue that there is still likely to be a significant gender difference in the way in which this caring is perceived and performed due to previously ascribed characteristics (Milligan, 2005; Twigg & Martin, 2015). Apparently caregiving women view their role as natural, affective and a continuation of their previously held nurturing role and are likely to be highly involved in this role. Conversely men see caring as being alien and are more task-centred in their approach because of their experience in the external world of work and consequently have a greater likelihood of adopting boundary setting approaches (Twigg & Atkin, 1994). Similar gender differentials in approaches to caring have been noted in recent research which maintains that in order to minimise disruption to their lives and to cope with the often unfamiliar role of caring, older male spouses tend to incorporate this caring into their pre-existing management skills (Morgan et al., 2020). Respondents in this research did not always appear to conform to these gendered differentials in their approaches to caring. For example, Mrs Flude, a woman in an unhappy marriage, said that she felt that caring for her husband allowed her to finally be in control in their relationship, feelings far removed from the nurturing female motives identified by some feminists (Finch & Groves, 1983; Milligan, 2005). Nevertheless, it is significant to note that male spouses tended to talk at much greater length about this caring and the practical tasks performed. This is reflected in the much greater average length of interviews conducted with the male respondents in this research compared to their female counterparts and helps to substantiate men's pragmatic and workman like approach to caring referred to by Morgan et al. (2020).

6.2   A Culture of Coping

The unique nature of the management strategies used by older spouse carers and their diversity to those employed by younger counterparts suggest that factors unique to the later life course are needed to explain them (Morgan et al., 2020). Such explanations are provided by gerontological research which has found that older people are characterised by commonly expressed attitudes of personal resourcefulness and resilience (Lloyd et al., 2014).

6.2.1   Stoicism

Recently emerged concepts of the fourth age have addressed the way in which the transition to frailty and dependency in later life is characterised by attitudes of independence and stoicism and a corresponding resistance to receiving formal support (Lloyd et al., 2014). Thus as a result of their past history of independent living older people can regard the onset of disability as a source of humiliation and stigma and a disruption to their sense of 'biographical flow' (Morgan et al., 2020). Indeed, there is a long history of work in social gerontology that shows how older people engage in' identity work' in order to minimise the impact of disability and to readjust their sense of self to new circumstances (Langan et al., 1996). This process of readjustment is likely to be particularly significant for older spouse carers for it will not only involve their own sense of self but also their sense of self in relation to those closest to them (Barnes, 1997). While as Twigg and Atkin (1994) observe, spouse carers tend to see caring as a natural part of the marital relationship leading them to put a barrier around this relationship against the unwelcome intrusion of outside agencies. This picture of resourcefulness in the face of difficulties was expressed by many respondents in this research and related to various aspects of their lives. Thus, as it was seen in Chap. 4, it is significant that, in spite of their high levels of caring demands, none said that they were wholly dissatisfied with their role:

> Looking after her she's never been any trouble at all, she's not a demanding person, never has been. (Mr Cicourel)

> I wouldn't say that her illness has caused me any bother, inconvenience, yes, but that doesn't bother me. (Mr Tunstall)

Indeed in spite of the downsides of caring, many appeared to positively embrace the challenges that it brought to their lives:

In fact I don't dislike cooking do I. I like cooking and baking. On a day when she's not too bad and we can't go out, I'll find something to do like baking cakes and one thing and another. Oh I like baking yes, and house-work. (Mr MacLellan)

She was OK ill she was about 75, until then she did all the housework. I didn't find it very hard to adapt, I'm very adaptable, and it didn't bother me taking over. It's folk's attitude. It's men's attitude towards housework. You either get it done or you let it go to rack and ruin. (Mr Caplow)

Further evidence of this stoicism was apparent in the high incidence of the words 'cope' and 'manage' when carers talked about their lives and these words were always used in a positive rather than a negative context:

We get by, I can manage. (Mr Caplow)

I can cope. (Mrs Reid)

We're coping aren't we, we could be better off but it could be a lot worse. (Mr MacLellan)

We manage quite well. (Mr Phillips)

A consequence of this stoicism and culture of coping there was a general reluctance to seek outside help thereby potentially compounding the demands of their role.

6.2.2   *Financial Caution*

The general stoicism of respondents and the culture of coping that they displayed were particularly apparent in the way in which they managed their finances and the cautious approach adopted in doing so (Argyle & Warren, 2005). In accordance with this, in spite of their limited post-retirement incomes, no respondents claimed to experience problems with debt and all showed evidence of a cautious approach to money:

I have to watch every penny. (Mr Tumin)

Specific areas of economy referred to in the interviews commonly included leisure activities and car ownership:

We had one (a car) before he retired but after he retired he couldn't afford it. (Mrs Williams)

> I used to change the car every couple of years. I haven't changed the car for the past nine years, as long as it takes me from A to B to do a bit of shopping because that's all I need it for. (Mr Cicourel)

In view of the increased incidence of charging for services as a result of the consumerisation of the welfare market, supportive services for the cared for person were also a common source of economy.

Respondents, in an attempt to accommodate their reduced post-retirement income, also utilised a cautious or 'tight control' approach to money management in which expenditure was routinised and debt problems were subsequently avoided (Argyle & Warren, 2005). Thus many spoke with apparent pride and often at great length about their budgeting strategies:

> So the financial situation is that I get the money and everything that I spend has got to come out of that and I have to put it away every week and by the time I put everything away there is nothing left. (Mr Tumin)

> I pay my electric on a little card at the post office and I pay my gas like that as well, so I don't get a shocking big bill. (Mrs Phillips)

> I have to save for the gas, electric and telephone, otherwise I wouldn't have the money would I, if I didn't save for it. (Mr Caplow)

Allied with this financial caution was a struggle to accumulate savings:

> You see I've got a bit of money, the bit of money I've got is for funerals and this and the other, do you know what I mean, if I had to use it now then something happened, I don't like debts. (Mr Cicourel)

> We've just about got enough money to bury us. It was a thing with older folks, they used to worry about that because everyone cried shame on them if they weren't buried properly. (Mrs Phillips)

Moreover, in spite of the growth of the electronic economy many respondents did not use a debit or credit card and preferred to pay in cash:

> If I want anything, I save up for it and pay cash. I like to put cash on the counter, I always do and if I have bills to pay I pay cash. I know it's a silly thing but it's the way I am. (Mr Tumin)

> The kids said to me you ought to get a credit card, I said I'm not going to get no card, I'm going to pay in cash, if you don't like it you can lump it. I like it that way. (Mr Caplow)

This lack of access to key financial products could be a source of difficulty as illustrated by the experiences of Mr Tumin who was charged by the bank to write out a cheque as he did not have his own cheque account:

> So he says, why don't you open an account and I says well I don't have enough money to have another account for a cheque book. Anyway it's not very often I want cheques. (Mr Tumin)

The financially cautious approach employed by respondents is highlighted by the case of Mr Tunstall (Vignette 6.2).

Vignette 6.2: The Financially Cautious Spouse Carer
Mr Tunstall was a 91-year-old spouse carer and had formerly worked for the council as an accounts clerk. Due to careful pension planning, his current household income was relatively high and incorporated Attendance Allowance for his wife, two state pensions and his own occupational pension:

> I caught onto this very early on that I'd got to save for my old age. (Mr Tunstall)

Like most carers in the sample, he displayed a cautious approach to his finances and kept a close eye on his financial situation:

> I like to know just how much I have got in my account. I can even tell you what I've got in my bank account. So I'll often go to the bank to support the pension to keep us going. (Mr Tunstall)

However, in spite of his regular withdrawals from the bank, Mr Tunstall refused to use his 'cash card' to access his money:

> When they first started with these cash safes in the wall I went into town and there was a queue outside waiting to use the cash dispenser and it was raining and I thought, what the heck are they doing there, why can't they go inside the bank. People in there will look after them, they will get their money, but no. I'm not saying it's a bad idea; it's a good idea. But there are people on the watch and if they see you

(*continued*)

> **Vignette 6.2:** (continued)
>
> getting out any money they'll nobble you for it. That's happened
> hasn't it? I'm not saying that my way is the correct way to do it it's just
> the way I like to do it. (Mr Tunstall)
>
> Although refusing to use a cash or credit card, went on to detail
> his complex array of savings accounts, illustrating his financial acumen:
>
> I got a 90-day which pays a much higher rate of interest than the
> ordinary account. I've got a 60-day which I use and I don't have to
> keep it over 60 days because if you have over £5000 you can withdraw
> money as and when you like and I've got a post office savings bank
> account which I can call on if I want a few pounds. (Mr Tunstall)

The cautious financial strategies employed by older spouse carers such
as Mr Tunstall (Vignette 6.2) and the apparent exclusion from the electronic economy that accompanies it is commonly associated with restricted
incomes and a lack of eligibility for credit (Argyle & Warren, 2005).
However, as the experiences of Mr Tunstall highlight, for this sample of
respondents, this exclusion appeared to be largely a matter of personal
preference:

> A lot of things I will pay cash. I don't like these plastic cards, I've got one
> but I don't use it, a cash card. It's handy but I've never been used to it I
> think as we get older we don't take kindly to change. (Mr Tunstall)

An implicit rejection of the consumer culture was also expressed by
several other respondents:

> If you can't afford something you shouldn't have it. (Mr Caplow)
>
> Younger people tend to buy things whether they can afford them or not.
> (Mrs Williams)
>
> Young people want things now but we had to save up in our day. (Mr Wilson)

6.2.3   Generational or Age-based Specificity

There is a further question regarding this culture of coping and caution displayed by respondents. That is, the extent to which it is unique to their generation or is specific to their stage in the life course. Evidence to support both arguments was yielded by the interview transcripts. On one hand, attitudes exhibited by respondents may have largely been adhered to throughout their lives as a result of the acquisition of life experiences and socialisation unique to their generation. Thus it has been seen that carers often implicitly or explicitly referred to their upbringing or to being 'old fashioned' when explaining their behaviour:

> We'd been reared in a very strict way as far as money was concerned. I was old fashioned and just gave her the housekeeping. (Mr Hunter)

Moreover, the Protestant ethic rather than the contemporary culture of consumerism would have been predominant during their formative years with older people being brought up at a time of low material expectations when saving and thrift were virtues (Argyle & Warren, 2005):

> I was brought up in a very careful family and I was brought up in several periods of really bad times. (Mr Hunter)

> It's the way we were brought up. We've never had big wages, so you learn to be very careful. My husband's pension goes into the bank, so we have a chequebook but as I say we're comfortable, we're not absolutely destitute. I'm not saying that we've never had things that we haven't paid for weekly but we've never gone into anything that we couldn't afford. (Mrs Williams)

On the other hand, the behaviour patterns and attitudes found amongst respondents may have been acquired only in later life, due to age specific factors with many carers referring to their age when explaining their behaviour:

> I think this is the point mean when you're younger you think oh dear I'll have to give up that. But you find when you're old that you don't want it anyway. Too many clothes and going out for meals, we very rarely do because we don't want to really. (Mrs Field)

In addition to not wanting to go out or being "too old" to do so, the onset of ill health and disability in themselves and their spouse and limited post-retirement incomes were more specific factors alluded to when carers tried to explain restrictions on their lives:

> We manage. As I say we don't go anywhere. I haven't had any new clothes because I can't get out to get them you see. (Mrs Lane)

> We really enjoyed life but when you stop work and there's no money coming in – we haven't had a holiday for 6 or 7 years now. (Mr Phillips)

A third possibility could be that generational and age-specific issues combine to render older people more willing and able to adapt to adverse circumstances than their younger counterparts. Thus age specific factors such as the increased incidence of poverty, ill health and disability and the subsequent mobility restrictions and restrictedness arising as a result of this may give rise to their 'social disengagement' (Cumming & Henry, 1962). At the same time, in view of older people's general attitudes of stoicism, this disengagement may be accepted more willingly than is the case with younger people, rendering them likely to adapt uncomplainingly to adverse situations.

While these suggestions are speculative, it is clear that the potentially multiple influences on the experiences and aspirations of older spouse carers and older people more generally potentially undermine the narrow approaches adopted by progressive generations of gerontological thought. Instead it suggests that elements of all three generations need to be incorporated in order to gain a full understanding of older age. Thus, in accordance with traditional approaches to older age and social disengagement theories (Cumming & Henry, 1962), ill health and disability continues to have an important impact on the lives of older people and their likelihood of assuming a spousal caring role. While in accordance with second generation theories, issues of material constraint and limited post retirement incomes can have a similar impact (Arber & Ginn, 1993; Phillipson, 1982, 2013). However, rather than being the passive victims of adverse circumstances as these two generations of thought tend to imply, older people actively adapt to these circumstances and these modes of adaptation are influenced by cultural and attitudinal factors. While third generations of gerontological thought take account of these active modes of adaptation and the influence of culture and attitude upon them they tend to suggest that these are heterogeneous and 'free floating' as individuals narcissistically define their respective identities (Gilleard & Higgs, 2000). However, contrary to these suggestions, evidence suggests that these modes of adaptation are characterised by a high degree of commonality between older people who rather than wishing to disassociate themselves from age based identities often readily accept them. These issues are not only of academic interest, they also have important implications for service provision and its degree of compatibility with the particular needs and aspirations of older spouse carers and older people more generally. This and related issues will be discussed in the next chapter which focuses on access to external support.

REFERENCES

Andréasson, F., Mattsson, T., & Hanson, E. (2023). The balance in our relationship has changed: Everyday family living, couplehood and digital spaces in informal spousal care. *Journal of Family Studies, 29*(2), 719–737.

Arber, S., & Ginn, J. (1993). Class, caring and the life-course. In S. Arber & M. Evandrou (Eds.), *Ageing, independence and the life-course* (pp. 149–168). Jessica Kingsley.

Argyle, E., & Warren, L. (2005). *Older people and their money: Issues for policy and participation.* Cash and Care Conference, University of York. Retrieved May 24, 2023, from https://doi.org/10.13140/RG.2.2.13295.23209

Barnes, M. (1997). *Care, communities and citizens.* Longman.

Carers UK. (2022). *State of caring 2022: A snapshot of unpaid care in the UK.* Carers UK.

Cumming, E., & Henry, W. (1962). *Growing old: The process of disengagement.* Basic Books.

Fetherstonhaugh, D., Rayner, J., & Tarzia, L. (2019). Hanging on to some autonomy in decision making: How do spouse carers support this. *Dementia, 18*(4), 1219–1236.

Finch, J., & Groves, D. (Eds.). (1983). *A labour of love: Women, work and caring.* Routledge and Kegan Paul.

Gilleard, C., & Higgs, P. (2000). *Cultures of ageing: Self, citizen and the body.* Prentice Hall.

Langan, J., Means, R., & Rolfe, S. (1996). *Maintaining independence in later life: Older people speaking.* Anchor Trust.

Lloyd, L., Calnan, M., Cameron, A., Seymour, J., & Smith, R. (2014). Identity in the fourth age: Perseverance, adaptation and maintaining dignity. *Ageing and Society, 34*(1), 1–19.

Milligan, C. (2005). From home to 'home': Situating emotions within the caregiving experience. *Environment and Planning A, 37*(12), 2105–2120.

Morgan, T., Bharmal, A., Duschinsky, R., & Barclay, S. (2020). Experiences of oldest-old caregivers whose partner is approaching end-of-life: A mixed-method systematic review and narrative synthesis. *PLoS One, 15*(6), e0232401.

Office for National Statistics. (2023, February 13). Census 2021 Statistics, *Unpaid care by age sex and deprivation in England and Wales.*

Phillipson, C. (1982). *Capitalism and the construction of old age.* Macmillan.

Phillipson, C. (2013). *Ageing.* John Wiley and Sons.

Twigg, J., & Atkin, K. (1994). *Carers Perceived.* Open University Press.

Twigg, J., & Martin, W. (Eds.). (2015). *Routledge handbook of cultural gerontology.* Routledge.

CHAPTER 7

External Support for Older Spouse Carers

Abstract Drawing on the insights provided in previous chapters as well as on the perspectives of older spouse carers, this chapter will explore their perceptions and experiences of external sources of support. In view of the increasingly significant role of informal sources in providing this support, the chapter will begin with an overview of help from kin and non-kin. This will be followed by a consideration of access to formal help including hospitals, care homes, home based provision and support groups. There will also be a discussion of the multiple factors that can impact upon this access.

Keywords Isolation • Independence • Fragmentation • Formal support • Informal support • Gaining access

In planning interventions for older spouse carers, it is important to take into account not only the central caring relationship but also the presence or absence of supportive networks from informal as well as formal sources. Evidence from around the world suggests that older spouse carers can be extremely isolated from these external sources of support and tend to be caring alone during the last years of their life (Ornstein et al., 2019). The rest of this chapter will be devoted to the further exploration of this access to external support.

E. Argyle, *Inside the World of Older Spouse Carers*, https://doi.org/10.1007/978-3-031-61578-8_7

7.1   ACCESS TO INFORMAL SUPPORT

While much work has been done in the fields of gerontology to explore the informal support networks of older people (Phillipson et al., 2001; Twigg & Martin, 2015), research with a focus on older carers in general and older spouse carers, in particular, is much more limited (Wenger, 1990). However, the insights of more generic research into unpaid care suggests that contrary to postmodernist portrayals of the increasingly individualistic nature of care provision (Chap. 2), unpaid carers access to informal networks of help is, to some degree, socially structured.

7.1.1   Help from Kin

With regard to help from kin, the 'hierarchy of caring' (Qureshi & Walker, 1989), has observed the way in which this kinship help tends to follow a definite and gendered pattern with children being the most common source of support and with daughters being preferred to sons. Thus, Mr Caplow and Mrs Harris, both of whom had sons and daughters, were largely reliant on their daughters for practical assistance:

> My daughter always brings me a few things in and they will last me till Wednesday till my other daughter comes. (Mr Caplow)

> She does all the shopping, she collects our pension and the rest of the shopping I get delivered from the local shops. (Mrs Harris)

Sons and daughters-in-law tend to be 'second choice' carers, when daughters were not available:

> Our son helps; he lives just half an hour away. He does the shopping and the gardening and heavy housework and he takes us to the hospital and the opticians but he works (Mrs Lane) My daughter-in-law does the supermarket shopping. (Mr Hunter)

For those without children, nieces and nephews were commonly cited:

> I have a niece who does the heavy washing for me, the bedding and stuff. I don't have any family so actually she's a substitute daughter and she looks after us. (Mr Tumin)

Due to the death or health problems of older relatives, help from same generation sources such as siblings was rare:

My sister lives not very far from the church but she's not very well and walks with a stick so I don't see much of her. (Mrs Coates)

My sister died when she was 70 odd, I could have had help from her. (Mrs Gibbons)

Indeed, the process of ageing could lead to a general diminishment in informal support networks through such things as the loss of work contacts due to retirement, through the death or ill health of contemporaries and through respondents' own ill health and mobility problems. This isolation can be compounded by social trends such as geographical mobility and the large-scale entry of women into the workforce. As such, kinship support can often be minimal and sporadic with older spouse carers usually forming a relatively isolated and self-contained unit (Ornstein et al., 2019):

They've got their own problems; you can't expect them to do much. They might come in an emergency but then it's getting hold of them. (Mr MacLellan)

They are busy looking after themselves. (Mr Hall)

This isolation from wider kinship networks could be due, not simply to the lack of availability of such kin, but also due to choice, partly due to an unwillingness to 'impose' on relatives:

Well you can't expect them to give their lives up for you can you, they've got their lives to live and they've got their work to do. (Mr Caplow)

Or due to the positive wish to be independent:

We try to be as independent as we can. (Mr Hall)

We don't like to depend on anybody else. (Mr Tunstall)

As previous chapters have highlighted, this reluctance to turn to others for help has been found to be particularly apparent amongst older people, who tend to be characterised by strong attitudes of self-reliance and personal resourcefulness (Lloyd et al., 2014). As it has also been seen, this apparent social disengagement could also be compounded by physical pathology as well as by material issues such as transport, housing and the 'instrumentalisation' of informal caring relationships (Chap. 5). The impact of these material issues on access to informal support is well illustrated by the contrasting experiences of Mr Denis and Mrs Field (Vignette 7.1).

Vignette 7.1: The Materially Diverse Spouse Carers

Mrs Denis was 85 and Mrs Field was 82. Both had been looking after their confused and physically frail spouses for around ten years. Although Mr Denis had been living in the same rented one bedroom flat for 20 years, he had no contact with his neighbours with whom he was on poor terms:

> I don't get on well with them. Well this one over here, they've been here for nine years and they torment me – knocking and noise and loud music. (Mr Denis)

Since he emigrated from Jamaica several decades ago, he had also lost contact with wider networks of kin who still lived in Jamaica. Indeed, although he had a son from a previous relationship, he had not seen him for many years:

> I don't have any contact with him. Years ago he wrote and asked me if he could come over and stay with me but I said no, we didn't have the room. (Mr Denis)

These experiences contrasted to those of Mrs Field who had lived in her large owner occupied house for 50 years and was in contact with a few of her neighbours, one of whom worked as her 'chauffeur' in return for the use of her car. In addition, unlike Mr Denis, she was able to employ 'live-in' help when required in order to support her in the care of her husband and was also able to accommodate her three children when they came to visit:

> They are very good. They come up quite regularly when they can and if I need anything getting, I'm very fortunate. (Mrs Field)

The impact of material issues on informal support highlighted in Vignette 7.1 has been enlarged upon by Phillipson et al. (2001). It is thus maintained that there is a strong likelihood that the kinship networks of those on a low income are also relatively poor and therefore constrained in the type of help they could provide. Moreover, the largely practical rather than financial orientation of this help is less able to transcend the barriers of geographical dispersion and family and work responsibilities. Thus it is argued that the 'social convoys' of working class older people tend to be more subject to disruption and fragmentation in this respect.

7.1.2   Help from Non-kin

In recognition of the inadequacies of kinship based support, Phillipson et al. (2001) maintain that over recent decades, society has moved from an older age experienced within family groups to one which is more voluntaristic and shaped by non-kinship based personal communities. These include neighbours:

> Next door because Pete can't do anything and I'm pretty helpless there's a man and his wife and the man will do anything for me. The man comes and changes bulbs for me, he's very good. (Mrs Harris)

> I go out with a neighbour upstairs. His wife comes down and sits with her while we have a drink. (Mr MacLellan)

Local community organisations can also be an important source of support. For example, Mrs Phillips, who lived in a warden controlled housing complex for older people referred to Neighbourhood Watch:

> We're in Neighbourhood Watch round here. We don't pay anything to be in it but we make a bit of money by having a raffle, so there is somebody giving you help, you know. (Mrs Phillips)

Another respondent spoke of her local care home helping out when her husband fell out of bed at home:

> I couldn't get any help next door so finally I rang the nursing home up and they came straight away, a man and a woman. So they're always willing to help me even when I'm not paying them. (Mrs Coates)

However, although most respondents were relatively long standing members of their neighbourhood, practical assistance from non-kinship sources was relatively rare with only six households claiming to receive regular support from such sources. Consequently, it is logical to assume that, just as social trends such as the increasing entry of women into the workforce have undermined the kinship networks of older people, such trends have equally effected ties with younger, non-retired neighbours:

> They've either died off or left, there's only a few we know, they're all new and they work. If I stood at the gate, they'll talk to you and they'll say 'how are you' but that's all. They're all working, they're busy. (Mrs Lane)

Many respondents also compared their previous experiences of neighbourliness to their current situation. This could be due to the changing character of their neighbours and neighbourhoods and due to the fact that previous neighbours had either died or left:

> I wouldn't call it neighbourly, not like the neighbours we'd been used to in years gone by. They'll stand at the door and speak to you but they won't let you in. (Mrs Taylor)

> I know one or two but it's not like the old times. Things have changed, you don't know your neighbours. (Mr Carson)

Moreover, neighbourhood organisations were not always positively perceived by respondents. For example, Mr Caplow spoke of the way in which he felt excluded in his local community centre which was dominated by older women who he found to be unfriendly:

> Sometimes I don't see anybody all over the weekend. There's a community centre but even then you feel lonely because in communities you get cliques. I go down there sometimes on a Thursday to play whist but you still feel out of it. As I say I go down there every week, now and again and the majority are women, the majority of them are widows, but it doesn't do to press your company on anyone because they get the wrong idea. If a man starts pressing friendship they start thinking something else don't they. I went there yesterday. There were eighteen there and out of that eighteen there's three men. (Mr Caplow)

Like access to kinship networks, the inadequacy of non-kinship support is likely to be felt more keenly by lower socio-economic groups due to such things as lack of internet access and private transportation as well as the restrictions on housing mobility experienced by social housing tenants. These inadequacies have led some to suggest the need for various forms of 'interweaving' or 'shared care' in which formal and informal sources of support combine in order to facilitate the development of innovative approaches (O'Rourke et al., 2021; Wenger, 1990).

7.2   ACCESS TO FORMAL SUPPORT

Twigg and Atkin (1994) maintain that the relationship between carers and service providers is 'mediated' and 'structured' by the respective meanings and interpretations attached to the caring role thus affecting the response of society, welfare agencies as well as carers themselves. These assumptions tend to reflect the belief that the spousal caring role is normal and natural and therefore not in need of support, a view often shared by spouse carers themselves (Ornstein et al., 2019) with 75 per cent of older co-resident carers having no regular visits from a service provider (Milne et al., 2001).

7.2.1   *Hospitals and Care Homes*

Assumptions on the 'normality' of the spousal caring role are reflected in the limited access experienced by older spouse carers to hospital and care home provision with few respondents being willing to even consider the possibility of permanent care for their partners:

> There's no way she's going away permanent not unless she says so but from my point of view, no, it's out of the question. (Mr Tumin)

However, short-term stays in hospitals and care homes were regularly utilised by some respondents with such facilities being identified as crucial in reducing carer stress (Twigg & Atkin, 1994). In accordance with this, a few respondents were highly complementary about these services, as the following quotes on care homes reveal:

> To be exaggerating, it's a bit like utopia. It's also good for her socially because she can talk to other people which makes a hell of a difference. She can think about things for a week instead of being stuck between these four walls. (Mr Tumin)

> They really are very nice people. You hear so many things about homes. (Mrs Field)

Another carer spoke positively about the regular day care that his wife received in a local care home:

> With the three days that I have I'm able to catch up with things that I can't normally do because I have to follow her around making sure that she's OK. (Mr Carson)

Many others were less enthusiastic about hospital admission or care home-based respite. This lack of enthusiasm could be attributed to such things the culture of coping adhered to by many older spouse carers as well as the high degree of interdependence within the spousal caring relationship leading to a reluctance to be separated. Consequently, spouse carers often continued to fulfil a care-giving role after their spouse entered respite care and care-giving stress could remain high as a consequence of this (Argyle et al., 2010):

> Well I know she's not happy when she goes in these places, she's happier at home and that's it. We've been married getting on for 60 years now and we cope anyway. It's alright, respite, but the trouble is when she was in I used to go and see her nearly every day. If I didn't she'd worry herself to death, it's a damn sight worse chasing backwards and forwards, she's better off at home. (Mr MacLellan)

In addition to the culture of coping and interdependence within the caring relationship, a further reason for the apparent aversion to institutional care for their spouse could be the apparently poor standards of care provided in these settings. For example, such things as staff shortages and overprotective workplace cultures can lead to a focus on maintaining the physical safety of residents rather than on promoting their psychological and social wellbeing (Argyle et al., 2017a). As Mr MacLellan and Mr Hunter recounted on their experiences of private care home provision for their respective wives:

> They used to sit her in a chair with a television, a little one not much bigger than this and then just forget about her, leave her. Well if she sits there like that she'll probably try and get up and do something, she won't be watching telly all day long. (Mr MacLellan)

> They're only there for the money. Each room has a buzzer in to send for help, well as we sat there the buzzers went for five or ten minutes before

anyone going, it's no use complaining because from what you hear they're all alike. (Mr Hunter)

Similarly negative perceptions could be held about hospital care. For example, Mr MacLellan and Mr Cicourel spoke of the worsened physical state of their wives following hospital discharge:

Last time she was in hospital was five years ago and she will never go again, not unless it is imperative. Because last time she was in hospital it was for respite, to give me a break and that was for 10 days but each time she's been in hospital, every time she's come back she's been worse. Last time she had bedsores. Another time they turned her to one side and then forgot about her. (Mr MacLellan)

You see because she can't communicate, they left her and her face stuck to her pillow and when they turned her over the skin fell off the right side of her face. That's why for the past four or five years I haven't been on holiday. (Mr Cicourel)

Moreover the environmental disruption caused by respite care admission could give rise to a worsening mental state for their partners, especially if they had dementia:

I don't want her in hospital, that's the last thing I'd want her to do because in her state, that's the end. As you know they keep doping them up to keep them quiet and eventually it has the final effect. (Mr Hunter)

While the rapid discharge policies adopted by hospitals could impact on the carer if their spouse was sent home too early. As Mr Tunstall said of his wife's recent hospital stay which he felt had been prematurely terminated:

They didn't pay attention to what she was like. They gave her a poor examination. She was not really fit to come out, especially coming out to be cared for by a ninety year old fellow. (Mr Tunstall)

Consequently, rather being due to irrational and outdated cultural notions of the 'workhouse' commonly attributed to older people (Argyle et al., 2010), the negative attitudes held by many older spouse carers towards care in hospitals and care homes could equally be seen as a rational response to realities of an inadequate service. As it was seen in Chap. 5, financial factors, especially the costs incurred to the household as a result of care home stays could be a further deterrent to seeking respite care admission (Cooper & Harrop, 2023).

7.2.2   Home-Based Care and Support Groups

The above findings suggest the need for flexible and affordable sources of formal provision, aiming to support the cared for spouse at home (Argyle et al., 2017b). Domiciliary support such as community-based professionals and sitting services seemed to go some way towards meeting this need, offering a potentially regular and reliable source of help. In accordance with this, some, such as Mrs Phillips and Mr Tumin (Vignette 7.2) spoke positively about the help provided by professionals in supporting them at home:

> They put a ramp in for us and they put double-glazing in for us. They send down a chiropodist because we can't get to the medical centre you see and they cut our toenails for us and things like that. Oh they've been very good the Social Services. (Mrs Phillips)

Home care has also been found to be highly valued by carers for whom practical, low level assistance in the home was their overwhelming priority (Argyle et al., 2017b). However, the increased targeting of these services at the most vulnerable and at those who live alone combined with its lack of consistency and flexibility could undermine the value of the help it provided (Argyle et al., 2017b; Cooper & Harrop, 2023). For example, Mr Caplow complained that home carers were unable to perform housework tasks and Mr Denis described how such carers were unable to cater to his special dietary requirements:

> Home carers visit every day. But it's been changed because when they first came they were shopping for us but then men took over with the shopping and the carers still cooked but sometimes I have to do the cooking myself because of the kind of food I eat. You see, they can't manage that kind of food so I have to do it myself; I do my own cooking now. We eat sweet potatoes and yam and bananas. (Mr Denis)

The inflexible practices of home care providers illustrate how, contrary to the advocacy of flexible forms of support in the community, institutional practices can continue to prevail and client choice is often simply limited to taking the service on offer or refusing it, rather than having it tailored to individual need. As such, not only is the availability of social support such as home care increasingly restricted but its quality has also been compromised with Cooper and Harrop (2023) finding that two thirds of social care recipients were dissatisfied with the service they received.

As it was seen in Chap. 3, recent developments in community care have given rise to new forms of support for carers which recognise their potentially independent needs and their role as co-clients (O'Rourke et al., 2021). Most notably carer support groups have become increasingly popular. These can be freestanding or offshoots of other services and can provide a valuable source of information and mutual support. The two carers in the sample who were part of such a group, Mrs Reid and Mrs Lipset, were highly complementary of them and the advice and companionship they had gained from membership. However, others were less enthusiastic with most citing the practical demands of caring as forming a barrier to such membership and attending group meetings. As the following respondents said when asked if they were a member of such a group:

> No, I can't leave her for long so I just don't bother. (Mr MacLellan)

> No. There's not much point because I can't really get out to go to one. (Mrs Field)

As well as the general restrictedness arising from their highly involved caring responsibilities, further barriers to joining a support groups could arise from the unpredictability of their spouse's needs or the fatigue arising from intensive caregiving:

> It's a waste of time; to me it is, yes. You see the thing is when you start joining a group or whatever; we get back to the routine. They say, right, half-past nine or ten o' clock the meeting starts. There's a time and a place. That's a luxury, which I'm afraid I've learned to do without. I can't do that because I don't know how she's going to be tomorrow or how she's going to be this afternoon. (Mr Cicourel)

> To be perfectly honest with you, I find it very difficult to get myself into town. It's an effort when you're tired, it's a terrible effort. I know that sounds very negative but when you're very exhausted, all you want to do is go to bed, I just want to sleep. (Mrs Flude)

Attitudinal factors as well as practical constraints could be another deterrent to older spouse carers from joining such groups. For, they may not regard themselves as carers with Carers UK (2022) finding that around half of all carers did not immediately recognise their caring role. Moreover, their strongly held culture of coping (Lloyd et al., 2014) could run counter to the mutual self-disclosure that such group membership implies.

7.2.3   Gaining Access

The potential importance of attitudinal issues such as stoicism in influencing older people's access to help and support has been recognised by the cultures of care approach within social gerontology (Fine, 2015). This suggests the need for a greater recognition of these issues and the way in which they can influence older people's access to external support (Lloyd et al., 2014). Similar recommendations have been apparent in literature on unpaid care. Thus as Chamberlayne and King (2000) observe, the incidence of unpaid caring does not simply emerge from official welfare systems but is independently mediated by the cultural and attitudinal perspectives of potential service users. Central to this literature on unpaid care is the recognition that this care as an integrated activity that transcends the boundary between private and public domains (Tronto, 1993) and involves a complex interplay between formal and informal support (Morgan, 2018). Consequently, not only can the attitudes held by carers potentially diminish their access to supportive services but these services are themselves structured by the shared assumptions of service providers (Twigg & Atkin, 1994) as well as by the organisational, political and economic contexts in which they operate (Lloyd et al., 2014).

   With specific regard to older spouse carers this process can be seen in such things as the perceived inevitability of their role and their corresponding invisibility to service providers (Ornstein et al., 2019). While on a broad level, this structuring has been seen in the emergence of neoliberal approaches to welfare, the corresponding shift towards community care and the marginalisation of statutory responsibilities (Cooper & Harrop, 2023). The rhetoric behind these developments has been to promote choice and innovation through pluralistic welfare services. However, in reality it has served to effectively 'privatise' the 'social risk' of caring (Morgan, 2018) by potentially restricting access to these services and rendering them inappropriate to the needs of older spouse carers and older people more generally (Chap. 3). Thus, the fragmentation of formal support provision which has taken place as a result of welfare pluralism has led to potential 'care gaps' as well as a confusion amongst carers over what help was available to them and how to gain access to it (Carers UK, 2022):

I have a very short memory and I get confused about what services are available. (Mrs Flude)

While the consumerisation of these services and the increased incidence of charging and means testing can form a further barrier to access (Cooper & Harrop, 2023), and runs counter to older people's preference for low level, accessible and universalistic forms of support (Cooper & Harrop, 2023). For example, Mr Caplow explained how he stopped his wife's home carers, as he was unwilling to pay the weekly fee:

I stopped that because I couldn't afford to pay them. (Mr Caplow)

Consequently, the words 'struggle' and 'fight' were used by a few respondents when recounting the process of gaining access:

We've got a stair-lift, which the social service put in after a struggle. (Mrs Gibbons)

In the beginning I really had to struggle, I didn't know who to turn to. My son used to have to pick him up when he fell over but now I'd know to call an ambulance. It sounds obvious but when you've never experienced it before. (Mrs Flude)

Such lack of information also raises concerns about the ability of carers to make informed choices about the most appropriate solutions for themselves and those for whom they care. For example, as Mr Cicourel described his attempts to obtain a home sitting service for his wife who had multiple sclerosis:

She said, how many times a week do you want help and I said 'whatever' and she said, how about a couple of times a week and I said yes that would be great. A week after she rang and said 'I'm ever so sorry but I'm afraid that you don't qualify because your wife isn't old enough'. (Mr Cicourel)

This confusion can promote a subsequent reliance on relevant professionals for guidance, undermining the principles of empowerment and user led provision upon which welfare pluralism was supposed to be based (Chap. 3). For example, Mrs Flude described how, after remaining unsupported for several years, she was forced to turn to her GP and then a social worker to help to guide her through the maze of formal provision:

In the end I went round to the practice (GP) and beat my fist on the desk...the key to the whole thing is a social worker, these things don't come to you other than through a social worker. That's the key, to have a social worker who is like, your ambassador, your mentor really, without a social worker I'd be in the dark. (Mrs Flude)

Moreover, the focus on user led involvement and 'shopping around' for services is potentially incompatible with the physical needs of older people for whom the onset of ill health and disability tends to be sudden and who also tend to recover at a slower rate than younger counterparts. It also runs counter to the innate stoicism apparent amongst older people (Lloyd et al., 2014) who may be unwilling to 'push themselves forward' and proactively pursue support (Twigg & Atkin, 1994). In accordance with this, initial access to formal support for older people is commonly initiated by welfare professionals following a crisis situation such as hospital admission:

I think how it came about was me having a bad heart. They asked me all these questions. I said my wife has to see to me the best she can and I see to her. It snowballed from there. They have welfare workers in hospital and they came to see me, they thought it was necessary for this to happen. (Mr Hall)

Yes, the care workers and social worker started through me having to go into hospital for an operation. (Mr Tumin)

Such access can also be initiated by relatives, possibly with a view to alleviating the potential burden on themselves as well as on the spouse carer:

It was my daughter. My daughter said I needed to do something about it, she said you're not going to manage. Just before Christmas I went down to the doctor. I thought I had flu but I had to have a pacemaker fitted. I've got diabetes as well, so it pushed things along and my daughter said I can't look after her (his wife). So they came to assess her and it started straight away. (Mr Carson)

The tendency for older people to access formal support only when a crisis point is reached and the common need for prompting and persuasion from others in initiating this access suggests the need for preventative, progressive and proactive approaches to the introduction of support (McGarry & Arthur, 2001). The success of this type of approach is well illustrated by the case of Mr Tumin who was initially reluctant to accept help in the care of his wife (Vignette 7.2).

Vignette 7.2: The Initially Resistant Welfare Recipient

Mr Tumin was an 84-year-old man who had been looking after his wife since she first became ill around three years ago. She experienced a variety of problems including confusion and minor strokes. Mr Tumin also had his own health problems including osteoarthritis and mobility impairment as a result of a hip replacement. He had always been reluctant to accept help from outside sources and first came into contact with formal provision when he had to go into hospital and needed support for his wife while he was away. This led him to be allocated a social worker who followed up his hospital discharge and persuaded him to accept home care and respite care for his wife:

> They were getting on to me and I was laying the law down as I saw it. There was Julie my social worker, two more ladies and a nurse I think she was a district nurse and then the two carers so I had four women I had no chance had I? (Mr Tumin)

In subsequent years, Mrs Tumin has received increased amounts of support and now goes in to respite care every five weeks about which Mr Tumin was highly complementary:

> I'll be quite candid, its luxury. There's a single bedroom on suite with a television in it, you can't get more luxurious than that and the food is absolutely fantastic. She says it's like a first class hotel for the food. The carers are out of this world and so are the medical staff. I said, 'so you'll come back here again?' And she said, 'oh yes', she wouldn't hesitate. (Mr Tumin)

Consequently, in spite of these initial 'pressure tactics', Mr Tumin was very pleased with the services he subsequently received, as he said about his social worker:

> Oh she's fantastic, really fantastic. I can't praise her enough. I only have to get on the phone and she's here, she comes of her own accord sometimes. (Mr Tumin)

The experiences of Mr Tumin (Vignette 7.2) suggest that, through the relevant adaptation of interventions and approaches, it is possible to overcome the multiple barriers to accessing external support provision experienced by older spouse carers. For the role of supportive services in shaping as well as responding to the experiences needs of older spouse carers and older people more generally Lloyd et al. (2014) indicate that more appropriate forms of intervention could lead to positive outcomes for these groups. In order for this to be achieved, greater understanding is needed of their experiences of this support, the identification of any unmet needs (Milne et al., 2001) and the adoption of a more culturally sensitive approach to service provision rather than the undifferentiated and 'off the peg' approach that currently prevails (Fine, 2015). It will be the purpose of the final chapter to further explore these issues and to make recommendations for an eclectic and integrated approach to understanding and responding to the needs of older spouse carers.

References

Argyle, E., Downs, M., & Tasker, J. (2010). *Continuing to care for people with dementia: Irish family carers' experience of their relative's transition to a nursing home.* Alzheimer Society of Ireland.

Argyle, E., Dening, T., & Bartlett, P. (2017a). Space the final frontier: Outdoor access for people living with dementia. *Aging and Mental Health, 21*(10), 1005–1006.

Argyle, E., Kelly, T., Gladman, J., & Jones, R. (2017b). The effective ingredients of social support at home for people with dementia: A literature review. *Journal of Integrated Care, 25*(2), 110–119.

Carers UK. (2022). *State of caring 2022: A snapshot of unpaid care in the UK.* Carers UK.

Chamberlayne, P., & King, A. (2000). *Cultures of care: Biographies of carers in Britain and the two Germanies.* Policy Press.

Cooper, B., & Harrop, A. (2023). *Support guaranteed: The roadmap to a national care service.* Fabian Society.

Fine, M. (2015). Cultures of care. In J. Twigg & W. Martin (Eds.), *Routledge handbook of cultural gerontology* (pp. 269–276). Routledge.

Lloyd, L., Calnan, M., Cameron, A., Seymour, J., & Smith, R. (2014). Identity in the fourth age: Perseverance, adaptation and maintaining dignity. *Ageing and Society, 34*(1), 1–19.

McGarry, J., & Arthur, A. (2001). Informal caring in late life: A qualitative study of the experiences of older carers. *Journal of Advanced Nursing, 33*(2), 182–189.

Milne, A., Hatzidimitriadou, E., Chrissanthopoulou, C., & Owen, T. (2001). *Caring in later life: Reviewing the role of older carers.* Help the Aged.

Morgan, F. (2018). The treatment of informal care-related risks as social risks: An analysis of the English care policy system. *Journal of Social Policy, 47*(1), 179–196.

O'Rourke, G., Lloyd, L., Bezzina, A., Cameron, A., Jessiman, T., & Smith, R. (2021). Supporting older co-resident carers of older people – The impact of care act implementation in four local authorities in England. *Social Policy and Society, 20*(3), 371–384.

Ornstein, K., Wolff, J., Bollens-Lund, E., Rahman, O. K., & Kelley, A. (2019). Spousal caregivers are caregiving alone in the last years of life. *Health Affairs, 38*(6), 964–972.

Phillipson, C., Bernard, M., Phillips, J., & Ogg, J. (2001). *The family and community life of older people.* Routledge.

Qureshi, H., & Walker, A. (1989). *The caring relationship.* Macmillan.

Tronto, J. (1993). *Moral boundaries: A political argument for an ethic of care.* Routledge.

Twigg, J., & Atkin, K. (1994). *Carers perceived.* Open University Press.

Twigg, J., & Martin, W. (Eds.). (2015). *Routledge handbook of cultural gerontology.* Routledge.

Wenger, G. (1990). Elderly carers: The need for appropriate intervention. *Ageing and Society, 10*, 197–219.

CHAPTER 8

Overcoming the Marginalisation of Older Spouse Carers

Abstract This concluding chapter will provide an overview of preceding content and consider its implications for research, policy and practice. The first part of the chapter will aim to challenge the fragmentation in perspective and focus that has tended to characterise approaches to unpaid care and older age. In doing so, it will advocate the adoption of an integrated approach to understanding the experiences of older spouse carers and in effectively responding to their support needs and aspirations. This will be followed in the second section of the chapter by a consideration of specific ways in which this approach can be achieved.

Keywords Culture • Constraint • Commonality • Integrated approach • Social risk • Precarity

In focusing on older spouse carers, a central theme of this book has been to challenge the traditional perception of older people as the passive recipients of care rather than the active providers of it, as well as making recommendations on the best ways in which they can be supported. For in spite of alarmist claims of a care giving crisis arising as a result of ageing populations, older people play a significant role in the care of others especially within the spousal relationship and their experiences vary significantly to those of younger counterparts (Morgan et al., 2020). Thus as it has been seen in preceding chapters, such carers tend to be characterised by high levels of involvement and interdependence within the caring relationship, display a high degree of stoicism and experience major role transformations in adapting to and managing their role. Combined with this is the 'double jeopardy' they often experience as a result of caring while dealing with their own health problems (Morgan et al., 2020). It has also been seen that in spite of these high demands, they have been neglected by researchers and service providers with policy and practice developments tending to directly or indirectly marginalise or run counter to their unique needs and experiences. Contrasting with the unique nature of caring in older age is the commonality in the experiences of older spouse carers across the world, which indicates the widespread relevance of these issues and their potentially international generalisability (Murray et al., 1999). While the persisting incidence of coupledom within older age groups, whether married or not (Office for National Statistics, 2023), combined with the erosion of external sources of support means that future generations of older carers are increasingly likely to be involved in less traditional but equally demanding dyadic caring relationships .

8.1   TRANSCENDING DIVIDES AND DISCONNECTIONS

8.1.1   *Fragmentation*

In addition to exploring the unique experiences of older spouse carers, a further aim of this book has been to challenge the divides that have characterised research into older age and unpaid caring. These divides have led to a general lack of integration between these two subject areas, while the fragmentation in the focus and approaches adopted by research in both of these areas has further undermined the value of the insights provided. With regard to research into unpaid care, as it was shown in Chap. 2, its focus has often been diffuse and ideologically bound, exploring many different aspects of caring and the experiences of different groups of carers but not usually those of older spouse carers (Morgan et al., 2020). Similar fragmentation has been apparent in the way in which this research has been carried out and in the paradigmic frameworks adopted (Purkis & Ceci, 2015), which reflect the methodological perspectives of positivism on one hand and phenomenology on the other. This methodological division has led to a narrow focus which has undermined the full understanding of the complexities of unpaid care, its multi-dimensional nature and the reciprocal exchanges taking place within the caring relationship (Larkin, 2017; Tronto, 1993). These omissions are further compounded by the false divide often placed between the interests of those within this relationship (Barnes, 1997).

Research into unpaid care has also tended to treat the experience of caregiving as isolatable from other aspects of life leading to a neglect of its social risks (Morgan, 2018) and the material, organisational and cultural worlds in which it is located (Purkis & Ceci, 2015). Thus research attempting to quantify the 'costs' of caring has neglected the influence of pre-existing contexts and circumstances on these costs and the disproportionate impact of these costs on different social groups. Similarly, although the growth of qualitative research into unpaid caring has helped to address the neglect of meaning and action apparent in quantitative studies on the issue, such research often overlooks the way in which these meanings and actions are themselves structured and constrained by objective social forms (Larkin et al., 2019). As Beresford (2002) observes, the growth of participatory approaches, particularly in qualitative research in health and social care has had a similar impact. For although such approaches have aimed to emancipate and empower participants, they have also neglected the wider context of inequality within which the research takes place and the systematic differences that can arise from this.

Like research into unpaid caring, similar fragmentation and division has been apparent in gerontological research. For in their rejection of the perspectives that preceded them, the varying insights provided by each generation of thought have often remained largely disconnected (Twigg & Martin, 2015). Thus, as it was seen in Chap. 2, early research has tended to adhere to a medicalised and individualised approach which emphasises the incidence of ill health, social disengagement and dependency in older age (Cumming & Henry, 1962). This pathologising view has subsequently been challenged by second generation approaches that highlight the structural basis and social construction of this dependency (Phillipson, 1982, 2013). In contrast, third generation, postmodernist approaches as well as concepts of cultural gerontology and cultures of care (Fine, 2015) have emphasised the diverse, active and meaningful aspects of behaviour in later life and minimised the incidence of this dependency (Gilleard & Higgs, 2000). This focus on culture in later life reverses a long standing reluctance to engage with this issue within social research, possibly due to a wish to avoid culturally determinist and pathologising approaches espoused by social theorists such as Oscar Lewis (1998). While as Twigg and Martin

(2015) maintain, the corresponding minimisation of dependency and physical decline in older age is indicative of a similar neglect of this topic within social gerontology due to the wish to avoid the biological determinism characteristic of early medicalised approaches (Cumming & Henry, 1962).

This minimisation of decline and dependency in older age has since been countered by concepts of the fourth age (Gilleard & Higgs, 2010) and of embodiment in later life (Tulle, 2015). However, as it was discussed in Chap. 2, due to the rejection by third generation approaches of the social determinism of the preceding generations, there has been an inadequate recognition of the ways in which the fourth age and embodiment are socially mediated and constructed (Grenier et al., 2017, 2021). While the increased focus on diversity and subjectivity that has been associated with third generation approaches has led to a similar neglect of the contextual factors and objective conditions which can have a significant impact on older people's lives, attitudes and experiences. Moreover, in spite of the emphasis of these third generation approaches on action and meaning there has been a general lack of understanding of the perceptions of those experiencing the transition to the fourth age. Although these knowledge gaps have begun to be addressed within wider gerontological research (Lloyd et al., 2014), relatively little is known about the way in which these transitions are experienced and managed by older carers or the best way in which policy and practice should respond to their needs (Morgan et al., 2020). With a view to addressing these issues of fragmentation, preceding chapters have explored the multiple influences on the lives of respondents which potentially transcend the divides that have traditionally characterised research into older age and unpaid caring. These are summarised below in relation to the three generations of thought that have been alluded to throughout this book and their respective concerns with dependency and decline, structure and constraint and activity and meaning.

8.1.2   *Multiple Influences*

In accordance with first generation approaches and their focus on decline and dependency in older age, the lives and experiences of respondents were greatly influenced by the incidence of ill health and disability both of themselves and of the cared for person. This incidence increased their likelihood of becoming a spouse carer and as it was seen in Chap. 4, all carers performed very demanding tasks as a result of the incapacity of their partner often while experiencing health problems of their own. Not only did this shared experience of ill health increase the demands experienced as a result of caring, it could also promote a practical interdependence within the caring relationship. This is illustrated by the vignette of Mr and Mrs Lane and Mr and Mrs Taylor (Vignette 6.1) who were all simultaneously the givers and receivers of care within their marriages due to shared physical impairments. In this respect, regardless of the influence of social factors on ill health and disability, it is indisputable that older people are more likely to suffer from such problems than younger counterparts with widespread implications for their lives. Even access to material resources such as cars could be mediated by such physical impairment as illustrated by the vignette of Mr Hunter (Vignette 5.2) who gave up driving due to his advanced age rather than as a result of financial constraint. Nevertheless, in spite of their widespread health problems and the demands of their caring role, in accordance with socially consensual perspectives and positive concepts of caring, most carers claimed to experience some benefits from this role and commonly experienced an emotional interdependence within it. This is well illustrated by the vignette of three former spouse carers who experienced a great sense of loss rather than a relief from burden when their spouse died or was relocated to a care home (Vignette 4.2).

In spite of the benefits that many carers claimed to experience, in accordance with second generation approaches, negative aspects of caring were also apparent. This can be seen, for example, in the accounts given by carers, such as Mr Carson (Vignette 4.1) on the stresses and restrictedness that they experienced when caring for a partner who had dementia. Similarly, the provision of personal care to their spouse could be experienced as alien and unpleasant rather than normal and natural as first generation and socially consensual approaches may maintain. It has also been seen that the experience and incidence of caring was socially mediated by such things as socio-economic status and the caring environment more generally. On a broad level this is apparent in the geographic disparity in the incidence of high intensity caring and the close correlation of this incidence with social and economic deprivation (Chaps. 2, 3, and 5). The social structuring of the caring role was also apparent in the responses of individual participants which revealed that limited access to resources could increase the demands and social risks of caring (Chap. 5). This could be due to such things as unfavourable living arrangements and financial constraint serving to reduce choice in the caring strategies utilised. This is shown in the case of Mrs Flude who would not consider care home admission for her husband with whom she had a poor relationship as she was reliant on his income (Vignette 5.1). Moreover, the consumerisation and instrumentalisation of external sources of support, as outlined in Chaps. 3, 5, and 7, could lead to a limited access to this support by the less well off as illustrated by the contrasting experiences of Mr Denis and Mrs Field (Vignette 7.1). Material resources could also influence the type of caring 'model' adopted and facilitate the adoption of boundary setting within the caring role as shown, for example, by the case of Mr Wilson (Chap. 4) who was able to pursue outside interests due to the availability of substitute care for his wife.

In accordance with third generation approaches, and their focus on action and meaning, as it was highlighted in Chap. 6, older spouse carers did not passively react to their circumstances but actively adapted to them. Thus they experienced significant transformations in their lives and a blurring of the role divisions adopted earlier in their marriages. Also apparent was a struggle for continuity or 'biographical flow' in the context of change which was particularly apparent in their accounts of their household routines. These modes of adaptation were influenced, not only by the increasing dependence of the cared for person or access to resources as previous generations of thought would maintain, but also by cultural and attitudinal factors such as traditional views of marriage, stoicism and a general resistance to formal provision. For example, a cautious approach to money management was widely expressed by respondents and is further highlighted in the case of Mr Tunstall who tightly controlled his household income (Vignette 6.2). While the commonly held resistance to formal provision was illustrated by Mr Tumin who had to be persuaded by his social worker to accept respite care for his wife (Vignette 7.2). However, contrary to the claims of third generation approaches, these modes of adaptation were not diverse and free floating but were characterised by a high degree of commonality between older spouse carers. Moreover, in spite of rhetoric towards culturally sensitive service provision, this adaptation tended to be incompatible with neo-liberal approaches to this provision (Chaps. 3 and 7). For the focus of such approaches on diversity, welfare consumerism and user led procedures could magnify the social marginality of older spouse carers and run counter to their commonly held stoicism and interdependence within the caring relationship.

8.1.3 Towards an Integrated Approach

In view of these diverse influences on the experiences of older spouse carers, a similarly eclectic approach is suggested in order to understand these experiences. Such an approach should incorporate elements of different generations of thought and include consideration of meaning and action on one hand and structure and constraint on the other. Thus with regard to gerontological theory, second-generation approaches provide a good basis for understanding the role of context and resources in structuring the lives of older people. They must however be supplemented by first generation approaches in order to understand the role of physical pathology in mediating this structure. In addition, third generation approaches are also required in order that the meaningful aspects of older people's lives are taken account of and the way in which they actively negotiate social structures is understood and recognised. On a theoretical level an example of this integrated approach is provided by the concept of precarity within social gerontology (Grenier et al., 2017, 2021). For while this approach recognises the incidence of disability and dependency in the fourth age of life, it also takes account of the ways in which this can be socially constructed and encourages a greater recognition of both the meaning of care as well as the shared responsibility for it (Tronto, 1993).

Overlapping with this recently emerged concept of precarity within social gerontology is the concept of social risk within unpaid care (Morgan, 2018). This recognises the potentially socially constructed nature of this risk and takes account of the material, organisational and cultural worlds that can influence caregiving (Fine, 2015; Purkis & Ceci, 2015). In the light of these observations, Beresford (2002) advocates the adoption of an 'emancipatory' research paradigm within health and social care research. Unlike participatory approaches, this emancipatory approach should take account of wider social structures and aim for reciprocity, gain and empowerment in the research relationship. As it was suggested in Chaps. 2 and 3, in order to explore both the meaningful and the structured aspects of human experience, both qualitative and quantitative methods should be used in these investigations with the strengths of one helping to compensate for the weaknesses of the other. Along similar lines, Larkin et al. (2019, 2022) suggest the adoption of a new paradigm termed 'understanding and applying'. This would involve a fusion of approaches which brings together analysis and perspectives from different sources in order to generate new knowledge and insights on which to base coherent and sustainable developments in policy and practice.

Similar integration and adaptation is needed in policy and practice interventions which have failed to respond to the unique needs of older spouse carers. For a 'one size fits all' approach to welfare support is not appropriate when addressing these needs, nor does it address the possibility of service development in order to meet their unmet needs (Johansson et al., 2022). In recognition of the interdependence between paid and unpaid care within the welfare partnership (Tronto, 1993), a 'multipronged' approach should be adopted which focuses on both of these aspects of care. While in view of the common interests shared by carers and care receivers for adequate help, these interventions should be aimed at the care receiver as well as the care giver. In accordance with this and with a view to addressing the false dichotomy placed by policy between the respective interests and identities of care givers and care receivers, Twigg and Atkin (1994) suggest that a 'superseded carer' model be adopted which would aim to transcend the caregiving relationship. Drawing on the philosophy of care ethics, this issue is enlarged upon by Tronto (1993) who offers an 'ideal type' model of care as an integrated practice comprised of four phases which include 'caring about', 'taking care of', 'care giving' and 'care receiving'. As such, not only does it locate the cared for person as an active agent in the practice of care but it also advocates a shared responsibility for this care beyond the caring dyad and provides a framework through which that shared responsibility can manifest itself within policy and practice (O'Rourke et al., 2021). A major benefit of these recommendations is in their breadth of impact. For, in their recognition of the shared needs of carers and receivers, they would potentially lead to positive outcomes both for older people in need of care as well as for those providing this care.

The implementation of such measures might seem to be a challenging expectation, especially in view of the long standing neglect and marginalisation of older spouse carers as well as the long recognised barriers to the implementation of change in health and social care settings (Harnett et al., 2021). However, recent developments suggest that this implementation may be increasingly achievable. For although the transition from care *in* the care *by* the community described in Chap. 3 is often seen in a negative light serving to compound the demands on carers and reduce costs to the state, community based approaches often see this transition as a potentially positive development. For it can promote flexibility and responsiveness in the support provided which is further reflected in the fluidity of concepts of the fourth age and cultures of care and the dynamic interplay between formal and informal support provision that they portray (Lloyd et al., 2014). Moreover, in spite of the need for a bespoke approach to older spouse carers (Johansson et al., 2022), rather than 'reinventing the wheel', relevant service developments can potentially draw upon existing innovative practice and incorporate elements of successive generations of thought as outlined in Chaps. 2 and 3. These include individualised case-work and universalistic forms of basic and easily accessible support as advocated by first generation approaches (Clarkson et al., 2018; Hsieh et al., 2022). While in accordance with third generation and neo-liberal concepts of activity and involvement, initiatives involving care for older people by older people, self-help and shared care are recommended by some (Hou & Kuo, 2021; OECD, 2020). Finally, in view of the social construction of older age and unpaid caring, more radical, collectivised and community based strategies would also seem to be appropriate (Carers UK, 2023; Cooper & Harrop, 2023). Such approaches can be associated with second generation perspectives on society and the state and aim to recognise and address broader societal issues rather than simply focusing on the individual (Phillipson, 1982, 2013).

8.2   Inclusive Approaches

8.2.1   Integrated Services

As it has been seen in preceding content, policy trends towards welfare pluralism and the service fragmentation that has arisen from this can potentially form a barrier to access (Argyle et al., 2017). This problem is particularly acute for older people who may be unable or unwilling to 'shop around' for services and who often endure multiple chronic conditions requiring attention from several providers across poorly coordinated health and social care systems (OECD, 2020). In view of this fragmentation and the problems of access and coordination arising from this, there have long been calls for the greater service integration and more collaboration and communication between different care sectors (Argyle et al., 2017). Indeed, coordination between health and social care sectors is the number one priority in the long term care agendas of OECD countries with one third of these countries having policies in place to support the better integration of services (OECD, 2020). It is felt that this would help to promote continuity and responsiveness in the care provided, reduce the need for emergency hospital admissions and delayed discharges and ultimately reduce the burdens on unpaid carers. For example in their Finnish study of older spouse carers, Turjamaa et al. (2020) suggest the need for overlapping, seamless, multi-professional and client centred support for older carers and their spouses. Several other countries are developing mobile hospital at home services either as a preventative means of avoiding hospital admission or as a way of facilitating the process of hospital discharge (OECD, 2020). Similarly, within the UK there has been a widespread recognition of the need to overcome the inadequacies that characterise the current system of social care and the development of interconnected support services which would be accessible to all of those in need of this support (Cooper & Harrop, 2023).

A recent example of such an integrated approach is provided by the National Integrated Care Programme for older persons in Ireland (Harnett et al., 2021) which was first established in 2016 in response to the needs of an increasingly ageing population. It adopts a multi-faceted approach to designing and delivering care across hospitals and communities and between providers, users and carers and aims for a transition from episodic and acute care to coordinated, longitudinal, and integrated models. On reviewing evidence on integrated care for older people, it found that such an approach could improve health and social care outcomes and the efficiency and effectiveness of service provision while also reducing carer burden. The most effective aspects of this approach were found to be bespoke care pathways, multidisciplinary teams working in the community and a case management approach. However it was also found that there tended to be major challenges in implementing such an approach deriving from the lack of conceptual clarity of the 'polymorphous' concept of integrated care as well as a similar uncertainty on how it could best be systematically implemented. With a view to addressing these challenges to implementation, existing insights were drawn upon and a ten step framework was adopted which ranged from establishing governance structures to the use of monitoring and evaluation.

8.2.2 Shared Care

Although the need for service integration is commonly associated with the health and social care sectors, it can also apply to the creation of better links between the formal and informal provision with an average of 30 per cent of older people in OECD countries receiving care from both sources (OECD, 2020). In accordance with this there has long been an advocacy for shared responsibility for care provision and a 'sensitive interweaving' of support between formal and informal sources (O'Rourke et al., 2021; Phillipson et al., 2001). Similarly, in view of the 'adapted intergenerational contract' which requires older people to take more responsibility for the care of themselves and their contemporaries (Harper, 2010), innovations involving care for older people by older people would seem to be appropriate. These could, through formal input, create and maximise opportunities for carers and former carers to engage in reciprocal help and, in doing so, emphasise the mutuality and human affirmation involved in helping each other. For example, Argyle et al. (2010) suggest that care homes should make greater efforts to elicit the involvement of former carers in care home life, potentially helping to alleviate the sense of loss that such carers often experience (Larkin & Milne, 2017). However, in spite of this long standing advocacy of shared care, less than half of OECD countries have implemented policies aimed at strengthening links between formal and informal sources of support (OECD, 2020). Moreover, evidence suggests a general degree of dissatisfaction held by formal and informal carers on their mutual collaboration as well as a lack of understanding and appreciation of their respective roles (OECD, 2020). In order to overcome these difficulties, some countries such as Australia and Belgium have begun to include unpaid carers as part of care teams while greater levels of training and financial incentives for such carers have also been recommended (OECD, 2020).

A further recommendation by the OECD (2020) is the promotion of self-help amongst older people through the adoption by service providers of preventative approaches which place an emphasis healthy ageing and crisis avoidance. An interesting example of such a preventative approach which is aimed specifically at the needs of unpaid carers is provided by carer cafes in Taiwan which involve the creation of collaborative links within their local communities (Hou & Kuo, 2021). These cafes were launched in 2017 by the Taiwan Association of Family Caregivers in response to the needs of the countries ageing population with those aged over 65 years old now accounting for more than 16 per cent of this population (Hsieh et al., 2022). Their aims are to improve the identification of carers and help them to recognise their own needs, to increase their awareness of and access to support services, to offer them a short break from caring and to encourage social responsibility in supporting caregivers more generally. Ultimately, it is hoped that a more compassionate society will emerge from these developments where caring for caregivers becomes a shared responsibility. Building on the concept of a sharing economy and on mutually beneficial partnerships with local coffee shops and corporate sponsors, the cafes use various approaches to identify and access unpaid carers in a culture that regards such caring as a familial obligation. These include reframing respite as 'talking over a cup of coffee' rather than a formal service and using a variety of formats to guide carers to information and resources. There are now over one hundred of these carer cafes around Taiwan providing flexible and community based support for unpaid carers.

8.2.3   Low Level and Accessible Support

Along similar lines to integrated and shared care approaches, there have been recommendations for the implementation of forms of support which are compatible with recipients own cultural traditions and preferences (Fine, 2015). Thus, as it has been seen in preceding discussions, the neo-liberal context of welfare provision tends to run counter to the needs and aspirations of older spouse carers and older people more generally for whom accessible and low level help is an overwhelming priority (Clarkson et al., 2018). As the OECD (2020) state, this help should be people centred and community based and should include support with the activities of daily living such as washing and dressing and the instrumental activities of daily living including cooking and cleaning as well as respite care and home adaptations. It should also be easy to access with Cooper and Harrop (2023) suggesting the need for the greater availability of high quality, preventative and open access community based services as well as charging reform making short term care free or, at least, more affordable. The benefits of 'mutual circles of support' and 'peer mentors' are also gaining increasing recognition (Cooper & Harrop, 2023; Harrad-Hyde et al., 2024). These can help service users and their carers to navigate the care system and to plan, implement and evaluate their personal goals. In doing so they help to enhance social connections and promote stability, advocacy and empowerment. They can also promote person centred and holistic approaches to care rather than the bureaucratic and formulaic approaches which tend to prevail (Johansson et al., 2022).

In addition to their preference for low level and accessible forms of support, a further characteristic of older spouse carers and older people more generally is their stoicism in the face of adversity (Lloyd et al., 2014). For older carers this is often accompanied by a reluctance to identify as a carer or accept support in this role. As O'Rourke et al. (2021) observe, this reluctance could be addressed through the development of different forms of access points that are shaped collaboratively with older people themselves. Carer resistance can also be overcome by service providers making greater efforts to identify them and by adopting swift, sensitive and proactive approaches in order to support them in their role and through the gradual introduction of low level help (McGarry & Arthur, 2001; Turjamaa et al., 2020). These measures would not only provide carers with respite from caring, they would also help to gradually overcome any initial suspicion held by older spouse carers towards formal service provision, avoiding the subsequent need for crisis intervention. An example of this type of easily accessed and basic support is provided by the integrated respite systems available to carers in Sweden where unpaid carers are offered 'in home' day time respite care free of charge as well as 24 hour 'instant relief' or weekend breaks. In addition to respite services, carer counselling programmes are also available and collaboration with carers is encouraged by service providers in order to create more 'carer friendly' institutions (International Alliance of Carer Organisations, 2021).

8.2.4   Campaigning and Community-Based Strategies

In view of the role of contextual factors such as government policy in potentially compounding the demands experienced by carers, wider campaigning and community based strategies are advocated by some. Such approaches run counter to the individualised approaches traditionally adopted towards older people and their carers which can serve to perpetuate pathological and medicalised perceptions of their needs. For example, in view of the common need shared by carers and care receivers for affordable and accessible help, anti-ageist practices are required which challenge the role of welfare provision in reinforcing the dependency and disadvantage of older people and their carers (Phillipson, 1982, 2013). The quality and quantity of social care provision also needs to be addressed due to years of underfunding (Cooper & Harrop, 2023). In response to this, the social care union, Unison have launched a National Care Service campaign. This aims to reverse the privatisation and fragmentation that characterises the current system of social care which it believes should become part of a nationally recognised institution and focus on providing good quality care for those in need rather than delivering profits. With this goal in mind it has identified ten 'building blocks'. These include such issues as models of support, access, affordability, rights and unpaid carers. It has also proposed the need for a National Care Service Act which expands and revises the Care Act 2014 which it is claimed has never been fully implemented due to resource constraints (Cooper & Harrop, 2023). A similarly broad approach is advocated by the Local Government Association (2024) who suggest the need, not only for better resourcing, but also for an end to the politicization of social care and the establishment of cross-party consensus in its operation.

As Cooper and Harrop (2023) recognise, in spite of the wide ranging and nationwide inadequacies of social support provision in England, it has not impacted all residents equally with older people in the most deprived areas being twice as likely to lack support compared to those in the least deprived. As it has been seen, similar socio-economic differentials are apparent in the incidence and intensity of unpaid caring with poorer groups being more likely to be performing a high intensity caring role than better off counterparts (Arber & Ginn, 1993). This suggests the need for various forms of targeted work in order to tackle social inequality and the inclusion of carers in programmes aimed at combatting this inequality (Carers UK, 2022). On a local level, this targeted work could adopt various anti-poverty strategies and encourage the involvement of neighbourhood organisations in tackling the social and economic disadvantage of residents. While on a broader level, campaigning work can also be an effective strategy. For example, in 2023, Carers UK launched a Carer Poverty Coalition (Carers UK, 2023) made up of around one hundred organisations as well as a small steering group of current and former carers. This coalition aims to campaign for better financial support for carers, helping them to escape from poverty and to lessen the financial hardship that they experience through improvements to the benefits system. It also aims to build awareness of carer poverty and the impact of the cost-of-living crisis on unpaid carers, helping to bring about policy change that appropriately values carers.

8.2.5   *Holistic Needs Assessments*

In spite of the condemnation of individualised approaches by some advocates of community based interventions, such approaches can still play an important role in addressing the needs of older spouse carers and in challenging the commonly adopted 'off the peg' approach to meeting them (Johansson et al., 2022). This is particularly apparent in the process of needs assessment which should help to establish a framework of intervention which is holistic in orientation rather than simply being a box ticking exercise. However not only do 'client centred' assessments potentially emphasise the conflicting needs within the caring relationship, they are also focused on the levels of need of the person being assessed and their ability to perform the activities of daily living (Barnes, 1997). As it has been seen, this focus can run counter to the stoicism of older spouse carers and the interdependence commonly found within their caring relationships, rendering them unwilling to admit to the need for support by themselves or their partners. As preceding discussions of research methodology have illustrated, it is likely that informal, conversational and relatively unstructured methods of assessment are more likely to get through older people's apparent stoicism and prioritise their own lived experiences.

Such methods also have the advantage of allowing the respondent to help to set the agenda, thus facilitating the development of inclusive forms of practice and service provision. These assessments should be an ongoing process and regularly updated as older people gradually come to terms with their need for support and carried out within the context of the spousal caring relationship. As such, Morgan et al. (2020) maintain that practitioners and policy makers should recognise the interdependence between older spouses and 'think couple' when designing strategies to support them. They should also develop new ways of engaging with older spouse carers who are often 'co-workers' in their partners care while also being 'co-patients' with health problems of their own. An example of such an inclusive approach is provided by Hsieh et al. (2022) in their Taiwan based action research study with the older adult spousal caregivers of people with dementia. The aim of this study was to develop a programme of support and empowerment for these carers by drawing on their own knowledge and perspectives and consisted of three stages. The first stage was to become familiar with the carers home situation through effective dialogue. The second stage was to confirm the daily needs and expectations of the carer and their spouse. The third stage aimed to enhance the interactions and quality of life of respondents and to further connect them to community resources to form a supportive network enabling the effective continuation of the spousal caring relationship.

8.2.6   Innovative Research

In addition to service developments, the unique but neglected experiences of older spouse carers suggests the need for more research into these experiences which, as it has been shown, cannot be extrapolated from those of younger counterparts. For while the study presented here has gone some way to redressing their neglect and aims provide a useful point of comparison for future research in the area, its scope has inevitably been limited by its relatively small scale and by the fact that all respondents were resident in one UK city. This limitation has been compounded by the emergent nature of qualitative research for, due to constraints in time and resources, emergent themes could not be fully explored. While, due to the process of sample selection, the carers taking part were already in contact with welfare services and were therefore likely to be relatively recognised and supported in their role. Consequently, in spite of the general commonality found by other research in the experiences of older spouse carers around the world (Murray et al., 1999), the experiences of the carers presented here may not completely reflect those of all older spouse carers. This may be due to such things as the different contexts in which this care takes place arising from the varying availability and receipt of formal support provision both in the UK and internationally as well as demographic, socio-economic and cultural differences.

In the light of these omissions, further research is needed, especially from a multinational and longitudinal perspective, which aims at unifying the diverse influences on the experiences of older spouse carers and the three generations of thought that have engaged in their exploration. For example, future research could explore the extent to which the attitudes and strategies found amongst older spouse carers (Morgan et al., 2020) and older people more generally (Lloyd et al., 2014) are generationally related and held throughout the life course on one hand or are specific to the later life stage on the other. While in view of the reducing popularity of marriage, similar exploration is needed into the extent to which the experiences of older spouse carers are unique to traditionally married couples or are also shared by unmarried older couples in dyadic caring relationships. Greater understanding of these issues would, in itself, help to highlight whether or not younger people will assume similar attitudes and approaches when they themselves become older with subsequent implications for welfare policy and practice. Similar exploration is needed into the complex interaction between structure and constraint on one hand and action and meaning on the other in the lives of older spouse carers and of older people more generally. For although the emergence of third generation perspectives have helped to challenge ageist assumptions and stereotypes (Twigg & Martin, 2015), their focus on diverse and subjective experience has led to a neglect of the objective conditions which can shape these experiences and the 'collective subjectivities' that can arise from them (Tanner, 2010). If these influences and contexts are neglected then there is a danger of reproducing the individualised and pathologising approaches of preceding generations of thought which have long been discredited (Twigg & Martin, 2015).

8.3   CONCLUSION

In spite of the increasing recognition of active ageing and the capacity of older people to lead socially and economically productive lives, they are still often perceived as being the passive victims of adverse circumstances. It has been an important purpose of this book to challenge this perception by exploring the way in which older spouse carers, who form the majority of the increasingly significant older carer population, experience and manage their role. It has thus been argued that this role shows great diversity from that of younger counterparts and is characterised by a high degree of caring involvement, interdependence, significant and stoical modes of adaptation and a relative isolation from external sources of support. A further purpose of this book has been to highlight and hopefully begin to overcome the fragmentation that has characterised existing research on older age and unpaid care. As it has been seen, this fragmentation takes place on a number of levels.

Thus, in spite of the many similarities in theoretical developments between the two areas, there has been a lack of integration between research on unpaid care on one hand and older age on the other. In addition, there has been a fragmentation in the focus and approach of research into unpaid care both in terms of the methodology utilised and the area of caring focused upon serving to undermine the scope and understanding of the issues explored. This fragmentation has also been apparent in gerontological thought with there being little integration between the three generations of this thought. Thus each generation has tended to focus on their respective concerns with physical pathology and dependency, the social construction of this dependency and activity and diversity, with little consideration for alternative perspectives. In its attempts to unify these diverse issues, the breadth of this book has been a drawback as well as an asset for it has limited the depth to which issues could be explored and as it has been discussed throughout this chapter, many questions still remain.

A further layer of fragmentation has been added by the apparent disconnect between academic insights on older age and unpaid caring and relevant service provision responding to these insights. Consequently, in spite of the richness of academic debate on culturally sensitive approaches to service provision as well as on the support needs of unpaid carers, few innovative approaches have yet to be manifested in policy and practice which aim to meet the particular needs of older spouse carers. This compares to the profusion of services aimed at other groups of carers such as young carers. Indeed, it has been suggested that not only has policy and practice failed to respond to the needs of older spouse carers, it has effectively run counter to these needs with the neo-liberal context of welfare provision either directly or indirectly marginalising them as a group. In order to address these shortcomings, a number of suggestions have been made on relevant and appropriate service interventions including integrated, shared and low level care, campaigning and community based approaches and holistic modes of assessment.

A particular advantage of these approaches are that they do not involve 'reinventing the wheel' but can draw on existing good practice and incorporate appropriate elements of all of the three generations of thought that have been an ongoing theme of this book. In transcending the false dichotomy placed by policy and practice between the needs of carers on one hand and care givers on the other, such developments also have the capacity to benefit older people in general as well as their carers. However, formal provision alone cannot compensate for the role of contextual factors such as material constraint and wider policy and practice trends in promoting the dependence of older people on unpaid carers while at the same time reducing the capacity of such carers to cope with this dependence. Therefore, intervention should focus not only on the provision of direct supportive services for older people but should also aim to address the wider structures of society which undermine their own and their community's ability to care.

REFERENCES

Arber, S., & Ginn, J. (1993). Class, caring and the life-course. In S. Arber & M. Evandrou (Eds.), *Ageing, independence and the life-course* (pp. 149–168). Jessica Kingsley.

Argyle, E., Downs, M., & Tasker, J. (2010). *Continuing to care for people with dementia: Irish family carers' experience of their relative's transition to a nursing home*. Alzheimer Society of Ireland.

Argyle, E., Kelly, T., Gladman, J., & Jones, R. (2017). The effective ingredients of social support at home for people with dementia: A literature review. *Journal of Integrated Care, 25*(2), 110–119.

Barnes, M. (1997). *Care, communities and citizens.* Longman.

Beresford, P. (2002). User involvement in research and evaluation: Liberation or regulation? *Social Policy and Society, 1*(2), 95–105.

Carers UK. (2022). *State of caring 2022: A snapshot of unpaid care in the UK.* Carers UK.

Carers UK. (2023). *Carer poverty coalition.* Carers UK.

Clarkson, P., Davies, S., Hughes, J., Xie, C., Stewart, K., Clifford, P., & Challis, D. (2018, September). Priorities for long-term care resource allocation in England: Actual allocation versus the views of Directors of Service and older citizens. *Journal of Long-Term Care*, 13–23.

Cooper, B., & Harrop, A. (2023). *Support guaranteed: The roadmap to a national care service.* Fabian Society.

Cumming, E., & Henry, W. (1962). *Growing old: The process of disengagement.* Basic Books.

Fine, M. (2015). Cultures of care. In J. Twigg & W. Martin (Eds.), *Routledge handbook of cultural gerontology* (pp. 269–276). Routledge.

Gilleard, C., & Higgs, P. (2000). *Cultures of ageing: Self, citizen and the body.* Prentice Hall.

Gilleard, C., & Higgs, P. (2010). Aging without agency: Theorizing the fourth age. *Aging and Mental Health, 14*(2), 121–128.

Grenier, A., Lloyd, L., & Phillipson, C. (2017). Precarity in late life: Rethinking dementia as a 'frailed' old age. *Sociology of Health & Illness, 39*(2), 318–330.

Grenier, A., Phillipson, C., & Settersten, A. (Eds.). (2021). *Precarity and ageing: Understanding insecurity and risk in later life.* Policy Press.

Harnett, P., Williams, P., Conroy, D., Mulligan, D., Hardiman, D., Kennelly, S., Barry, S., & Heavey, C. (2021). *Implementing integrated care for older people in Ireland; getting from complex challenge to complex adaptation.* Retrieved May 24, 2023, from https://www.icpop.org/_files/ugd/29601c_e3934d2468344 2e48963c10656c05f89.pdf

Harper, S. (2010). The capacity of social security and health care institutions to adapt to an ageing world. *International Social Security Review, 63*(3-4), 177–196.

Harrad-Hyde, F., Jones, G., Agarwal, S., Faull, C., & Birt, L. (2024). Could peer-mentors support families of care home residents to prepare for deterioration and end-of-life? An interview study with families and care home staff. *Health and Social Care in the Community.*

Hou, S., & Kuo, T. (2021). Carer café in Taiwan: An innovative model providing caregiver support for older adults. *Innovation in Aging, 5*(Suppl 1), 485.

Hsieh, C., Yin, P., Chiu, C., Hsiao, Y., & Hsiao, Y. (2022). Support and empowerment for older adult spousal caregiving of people with mild and moderate dementia: A participatory action research. *Healthcare, 10*(3), 569.

International Alliance of Carer Organisations. (2021). *Global state of caring*. Retrieved March 1, 2024, from https://internationalcarers.org/wp-content/uploads/2021/07/IACO-Global-State-of-Caring-July-13.pdf

Johansson, M., McKee, K., Dahlberg, L., Summer Meranius, M., Williams, C., & Marmstål Hammar, L. (2022). Negative impact and positive value of caregiving in spouse carers of persons with dementia in Sweden. *International Journal of Environmental Research and Public Health, 19*(3), 1788.

Larkin, M. (2017). Supporting caring and carers in later life. *Innovation in Aging, 1*(1), 1109.

Larkin, M., & Milne, A. (2017). What do we know about older former carers? Key issues and themes. *Health and Social Care in the Community, 25*(4), 396–1403.

Larkin, M., Henwood, M., & Milne, A. (2019). Carer related research and knowledge: Findings from a scoping review. *Health and Social Care in the Community, 27*(1), 55–67.

Larkin, M., Henwood, M., & Milne, A. (2022). Older carers and carers of people with dementia: Improving and developing effective support. *Social Policy and Society, 21*(2), 242–256.

Lewis, O. (1998). The culture of poverty. *Society, 35*(2), 7–9.

Lloyd, L., Calnan, M., Cameron, A., Seymour, J., & Smith, R. (2014). Identity in the fourth age: Perseverance, adaptation and maintaining dignity. *Ageing and Society, 34*(1), 1–19.

Local Government Association. (2024). *The Care Act 2014: Ten years on from Royal Assent*. LGA

McGarry, J., & Arthur, A. (2001). Informal caring in late life: A qualitative study of the experiences of older carers. *Journal of Advanced Nursing, 33*(2), 182–189.

Morgan, F. (2018). The treatment of informal care-related risks as social risks: An analysis of the English care policy system. *Journal of Social Policy, 47*(1), 179–196.

Morgan, T., Bharmal, A., Duschinsky, R., & Barclay, S. (2020). Experiences of oldest-old caregivers whose partner is approaching end-of-life: A mixed-method systematic review and narrative synthesis. *PLoS One, 15*(6), e0232401.

Murray, J., Schneider, J., Banerjee, S., & Mann, A. (1999). Eurocare: A cross-national study of co-resident spouse carers for people with Alzheimer's disease. *International Journal of Geriatric Psychiatry, 14*, 662–667.

O'Rourke, G., Lloyd, L., Bezzina, A., Cameron, A., Jessiman, T., & Smith, R. (2021). Supporting older co-resident carers of older people – The impact of care act implementation in four local authorities in England. *Social Policy and Society, 20*(3), 371–384.

OECD. (2020). *Who cares? Attracting and retaining care workers for the elderly*. OECD Health Policy Studies, OECD Publishing.

Office for National Statistics. (2023, February 9). Census 2021 Statistics, *People's living arrangements in England and Wales*.

Phillipson, C. (1982). *Capitalism and the construction of old age*. Macmillan.

Phillipson, C. (2013). *Ageing*. John Wiley and Sons.

Phillipson, C., Bernard, M., Phillips, J., & Ogg, J. (2001). *The family and community life of older people*. Routledge.

Purkis, M., & Ceci, C. (2015). Problematizing care burden research. *Ageing and Society, 35*(7), 1410–1428.

Tanner, D. (2010). *Managing the ageing experience: Learning from older people*. Policy Press.

Tronto, J. (1993). *Moral boundaries: A political argument for an ethic of care*. Routledge.

Tulle, E. (2015). Theorising embodiment and ageing. In J. Twigg & W. Martin (Eds.), *Routledge handbook of cultural gerontology* (pp. 125–132). Routledge.

Turjamaa, R., Salpakari, J., & Koskinen, L. (2020). Experiences of older spousal caregivers for caring a person with a memory disorder. *Healthcare, 8*(2), 95.

Twigg, J., & Atkin, K. (1994). *Carers perceived*. Open University Press.

Twigg, J., & Martin, W. (Eds.). (2015). *Routledge handbook of cultural gerontology*. Routledge.

GPSR Compliance

The European Union's (EU) General Product Safety Regulation (GPSR) is a set of rules that requires consumer products to be safe and our obligations to ensure this.

If you have any concerns about our products, you can contact us on ProductSafety@springernature.com

In case Publisher is established outside the EU, the EU authorized representative is:

Springer Nature Customer Service Center GmbH
Europaplatz 3
69115 Heidelberg, Germany

The manufacturer's authorised representative in the EU is Springer
Nature Customer Service Centre GmbH, Europaplatz 3, 69115 Heidelberg,
Germany. If you have any concerns regarding our products, please
contact ProductSafety@springernature.com

Printed and bound by CPI Group (UK) Ltd, Croydon, CR0 4YY

27/04/2026

02097563-0014